Sue Kay & V

Ana.

# American
# Inside Out

Student's
Book

Elementary

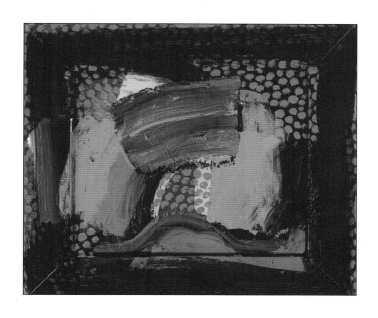

Macmillan Education
Between Towns Road, Oxford OX4 3PP
A division of Macmillan Publishers Limited
Companies and representatives throughout the world

ISBN 978 1 4050 1450 2

First published 2003
American Edition 2004

Project management by Desmond O'Sullivan, ELT Publishing Services.
Designed by Jackie Hill, 320 Design.
Illustrated by Cyrus Deboo pp. 71, 72 (b), 81; Rebecca Halls pp. 84, 85; Ed McLachlan pp. 61, 63, 64, 69, 72 (t), 73, 75, 76, 77, 82, 83, B90; Gavin Reece at New Division pp. 49, 54, 74, B86, B91, B92.
Cover design by Andrew Oliver.
Cover painting Patrick in Italy © Howard Hodgkin.

Authors' acknowledgments
We would like to thank all our students and colleagues at the following institutions where, with their help, we were able to try out our ideas in the classroom and throw out anything that didn't work: Susan Barber at the Lake School, Oxford; Ingrid Widdows and Steve Haysham at the Oxford College of Further Education; Faith Pritchard at Campsfield House, Oxford; Ceri Jones and Elizabeth Cowin at International House, Madrid. Also, all our friends and colleagues in the various Escuelas Oficiales de Idiomas in Spain that we visited or taught in, particularly Alejandro Zarzalejo and Araceli García Tubio at the EOI Las Rozas, María José Pi at the EOI Quart de Poblet, and Marisa de Dios at the EOI Valencia. A big thank-you to Mick Quirke and Manolo Grijalvo of Macmillan Heinemann Spain for organizing our teaching posts in Spain.
We are especially grateful to Philip Kerr for the Inside Out Workbook and to Ceri Jones for her contribution, to Helena Gomm and John Hird for the Inside Out Teacher's Book, to Pete Maggs for the highly successful weekly Inside Out e-lessons (now over 40,000 subscribers), to Guy Jackson for running the Inside Out Web site at www.insideout.net, and to everybody involved in the Inside Out Resource Pack—a great team!
At Macmillan Education, we would like to thank Sue Bale (publishing director) and David Riley (publisher). We would also like to thank Pippa McNee (freelance picture researcher), Alyson Maskell and Celia Bingham (freelance editors), Paulette McKean (freelance permissions editor), Xanthe Sturt Taylor (freelance phonetics writer), as well as James Richardson and Vince Cross (freelance audio producers), and last but not least, Jackie Hill—our wonderfully talented freelance designer. Many thanks also go to the Macmillan production and marketing teams who have worked so hard to make Inside Out what it is.
As Inside Out Elementary marks the end of the Inside Out project (for the moment!), we reluctantly take leave of Des O'Sullivan (freelance project manager). Over the past three and a half years that we have been working together, we have enjoyed and benefited from Des's humor, sensitivity, energy, drive, and sheer professionalism. We cannot speak highly enough of him—it has been a privilege to work with him, and we have learned a great deal from the experience. Much more than that, Des has supported us through all the ups and downs of work and life throughout the Inside Out project, often in ways that go beyond the call of duty. Thanks, Des—we couldn't have done it without you, and we look forward to working with you again in the future.
We would like to give a special thank-you to Michael Rundell, who took time from his busy schedule to provide us with the necessary data from the Macmillan Essential Dictionary to inform our Word list.
We would also like to thank Chris Campbell and Simon Dix (The Swan School, Oxford), Jenny Johnson (International House, Barcelona), and Beth Neher (Hammersmith and West London College) for their insightful comments, which have helped to make this a better book. Finally, we are so grateful to our families for their ongoing support and understanding.

This book, along with all the books in the Inside Out series, is dedicated to Mike Esplen, former managing director of Heinemann ELT. Thank you, Mike, for believing in us during those crucial early stages and giving us enough time and space to develop our ideas.

The authors and publishers would like to thank the following for permission to reproduce their material:
I Have a Dream Words and Music by B Andersson/B Ulvaeus, reprinted by permission of Bocu Music Ltd. Extract and photograph from "Letter From Karyn…" from www.savekaryn.com, reprinted by permission of RLR Associates Limited on behalf of the author. John Kitching "I Love Geography" copyright © John Kitching 2002 from The Works 2 edited by Brian Moses and Pie Corbett (Macmillan, 2002), reprinted by permission of the author.

The authors and publishers wish to thank the following for permission to reproduce their photographs:
Alamy pp. 50 (c, d), 66, 78 (l); Roderick Angle Photography p. 48; Anglia/Bob Hobbs p. 47; www.savekaryn.com p. 55; Jay Conely p. 68 (l); Corbis pp. 57, 58, 62, 70 (l), 78 (3), 79 (m, t), 80; Corbis/Jason Florio, p. 81; 4C's Enterprises p. 70 (b); Rob Fitzpatrick p. 68 (rt); FriendsReunited.com p. 67; Tim Friers p. 68 (rb); Image Bank p. 50 (b, e, g); Sue Kay and Vaughan Jones p. 46; Music Pics p. 50; Photonica Green p. 66; Stone pp. 50 (a, f), 60, 61, 70 (r), 78 (2, 4).

Commissioned photography by Haddon Davies p. 52.
Models provided by Elliot Brown and The Source Model agencies Oxford.
Thanks to The White Horse Sports and Tennis Centre, Abingdon.
Researched images sourced by Pippa McNee Picture Research.

Printed and bound in Thailand

2013 2012 2011 2010 2009
12  11  10  9  8

# Looks

### Vocabulary: description

**1**  Work with a partner. Read the information below and label the photos.

    a)  Will has a shaved head. He has a gold chain.
    b)  Jennifer has wavy brown hair.
    c)  Andy has very curly hair.
    d)  Jimmy has spiky hair and blond highlights.
    e)  Sue has dark hair and blue eyes.
    f)  Albert has short gray hair.
    g)  Gus has dark brown eyes and short hair.
    h)  Carla has wavy light hair and brown eyes. She's very pretty.
    i)  Ellen has dark medium-length hair. She has a lovely smile.
    j)  Nancy has short curly hair. She's very cute.

1 ____    2 *Will*    3 ____    4 *Gus*    5 ____
6 *Andy*    7 ____    8 *Jimmy*    9 ____    10 ____

**2**  Read the sentences in 1 again. Write words and phrases under the following headings.

| Hair length | Hairstyle | Hair color | Eyes | Other | Opinion |
|---|---|---|---|---|---|
| *a shaved head* | *wavy* | *brown* | *blue* | *a gold chain* | *very pretty* |

**3**  Add more words and phrases from the box to the headings in 2. Which words do you usually use: a) for women and men; b) for women only; c) for men only?

> long    straight    a mustache    green    blond    earrings    glasses    red
> beautiful    a beard    handsome    black    a tattoo    good-looking    a bracelet

**4**  Work with a partner. Student A: Look at page B86. Student B: Look at page B92.

**5**  Work with a partner. Describe people in the class and guess their identity.

For example:
*A: She has long straight hair and brown eyes. She has gold earrings and a bracelet.*
*B: Luisa.*
*A: Yes, that's right.*

**Vocabulary: *look(s) like*** **1** Work with a partner. Match the people on page 46 with the family relations (*a–e*).

a) a father and his son
b) a father and his daughter
c) a mother and her son
d) a mother and her daughter
e) a brother and sister

**2** Compare your answers to 1 with other students in the class. Use language in the box to justify your ideas.

> I think Jimmy/Will…looks like Albert.     They have the same smile/nose…
> They both have short hair/small ears…

**3** ▸▪ 59 Listen and check your answers to 1.

**4** Think about your family. Complete the following sentences so that they are true for you. Compare your sentences with a partner.

a) I look like ____ because we have the same ____ and…
b) I don't look like ____ because we don't have ____ and…
c) My father looks like ____ because they both have ____ and…
d) My mother looks like ____ because they have the same ____ and…
e) ____ look / looks like ____ because…

**Vocabulary: clothes** **1** Look at the photograph of Stuart. Check (✓) the items in the box that you can see.

**Clothes and accessories**

**Footwear**
shoes ✓   sneakers ✗   boots

**Dress clothes**
shirts   pants   jackets
suits   ties   coats

**Casual clothes**
tops   T-shirts   sweatsuits
jeans   sweaters

**Accessories**
belts   hats   sunglasses
rings

**Miscellaneous**
socks   underwear

**2** ▸▪ 60 Listen to an interview and underline the correct information. Do you know anyone like Stuart?

a) He has **35 / 50 / 350** shirts.
b) He has **100 / 200 / 300** suits.
c) He has **50 / 115 / 150** pairs of pants.
d) He has **25 / 100 / 125** pairs of shoes.

**3** Work with a partner. Except for *underwear*, all the words for clothes in 1 are in the plural form. Copy and complete the following chart.

| Singular | Plural |
| --- | --- |
| a pair of *shoes/sneakers*… | 2, 3, 4 pairs of *shoes/sneakers*… |
| a *shirt/jacket*… | 2, 3, 4 *shirts/jackets*… |

**4** Work with a partner. Look at people in the classroom. Add clothes to the list in 1 and write down how you count the words: *a XXX* or *a pair of XXX*.

# Mr. Average

Reading **1** Which magazines are popular in your country? Discuss with a partner.

**2** Read the magazine quiz about the average man. Take the quiz and discuss the answers with a partner.

---

## IMAGE QUIZ OF THE MONTH

**WIN A FABULOUS PRIZE!**

**1st PRIZE**
a weekend for two in one of the fashion capitals of the world, Milan

**2nd PRIZE**
1,000 dollars to spend in the clothing store of your choice

**3rd PRIZE**
a free one-year subscription to **IMAGE**

### MR. AVERAGE AND HIS CLOTHES

Choose the correct answers below.

How many items of clothing does Mr. Average have?

| | | | | |
|---|---|---|---|---|
| 1 | a) 32 | b) 22 | c) 12 | pairs of socks |
| 2 | a) 16 | b) 12 | c) 6 | pairs of underwear |
| 3 | a) 25 | b) 20 | c) 15 | casual tops |
| 4 | a) 13 | b) 0 | c) 8 | dress shirts |
| 5 | a) 21 | b) 12 | c) 7 | pairs of casual pants |
| 6 | a) 16 | b) 6 | c) 3 | pairs of dress pants |
| 7 | a) 2 | b) 4 | c) 8 | jackets |

How much does Mr. Average spend?

| | | | | |
|---|---|---|---|---|
| 8 | a) 550 | b) 350 | c) 250 | dollars a year on clothes |
| 9 | a) 140 | b) 90 | c) 40 | dollars a year on underwear |
| 10 | a) 150 | b) 50 | c) 15 | dollars a year on accessories |
| 11 | a) 300 | b) 200 | c) 100 | dollars a year on footwear |
| 12 | a) 1,500 | b) 1,000 | c) 500 | dollars a year on beer!!! |

Write your answers on a postcard and send them to Quiz, IMAGE, P.O. Box 1480, New York, NY 10016.

---

**3** Check your answers on page B90.

**4** Work with a partner. Refer to the *IMAGE* quiz and discuss the questions.

a) How many items of clothing do you think Mr. Average has in your country?
b) Who has the most clothes in your family?
c) How many items of clothing do you have (approximately)?

Numbers **1** ▭ **61** Listen and practice saying the numbers.

Numbers p. 116

> thir<u>teen</u>  <u>thir</u>ty    four<u>teen</u>  <u>for</u>ty    fif<u>teen</u>  <u>fif</u>ty    six<u>teen</u>  <u>six</u>ty
> seven<u>teen</u>  <u>seven</u>ty    eigh<u>teen</u>  <u>eigh</u>ty    nine<u>teen</u>  <u>nine</u>ty

**2** ▭ **62** Listen to four conversations (a–d). <u>Underline</u> the number of accessories each person has.

a) Hats: <u>14</u> / 40    b) Ties: 19 / 90    c) Rings: 15 / 50    d) T-shirts: 13 / 30

**3** Work with a partner. Listen and practice saying the first conversation in 2. Then use different numbers from 1 and practice similar conversations.

Vocabulary **1** Work with a partner. <u>Underline</u> the correct verb to complete the sentences.

a) I always **<u>get dressed</u> / get clothed** before I have breakfast.
b) On weekends, I usually **wear / dress** jeans.
c) I always **take out / take off** my shoes before I go into my house.
d) I never **put on / put in** sneakers to go to work or school.
e) I usually **change out / change into** casual clothes at night.
f) I always **try up / try on** clothes before I buy them.

**2** Which sentences in 1 are true for you? Compare your answers with a partner.

# The Oscars

**1** 🔊 63 Listen to a commentator, Ross White, describing people as they arrive for the Oscars ceremony. There is one mistake in each picture. Listen and write down the mistakes. Compare your answers with a partner.

ⓐ **Penelope Jones**

ⓑ **Melanie Matthews**

ⓒ **Kerry Fisher**

ⓓ **Bobby Finn and date**

**2** Match the verb phrases in column A with the noun phrases in column B. Who is doing each action, according to Ross White? Listen again and check your answers.

| A | B |
|---|---|
| a) I'm waiting for | her hand. |
| b) She's wearing | her car. |
| c) She's getting out of | her fans. |
| d) She's waving to | a beautiful blue dress. |
| e) He's holding | the big stars. |

# Close-up

**Present continuous**

( Verb structures p. B99 )

**1** Complete these *Yes/No* questions and short answers with a pronoun and the correct form of the verb *be*.

a) *Are* you wearing jeans?                Yes, *I am.*    No, *I'm not.*
b) ____ you sitting next to a window?      ____    ____
c) ____ your teacher standing up?          ____    ____
d) ____ the traffic making noise?          ____    ____
e) ____ the birds singing outside?         ____    ____
f) ____ you having a good time?            ____    ____

**2** 🔊 64 Listen, check, and repeat. Work with a partner. Ask and answer the questions in 1.

**3** Work with a partner. Student A: Look at page B86. Student B: Look at page B92.

## Language Reference: Present continuous

We use the present continuous to talk about activities in progress now.

| Question | Short answer *Yes* | Short answer *No* |
|---|---|---|
| *Are you waving?* | *Yes, I am.* | *No, I'm not.* |
| *Is he reading?* | *Yes, he is.* | *No, he isn't.* |
| *Is it raining?* | *Yes, it is.* | *No, it isn't.* |
| *Are the birds singing?* | *Yes, they are.* | *No, they're not.* |

Compare the meanings of the present continuous and the simple present.

*"What are you doing?" "I'm planning my lessons."* (in progress now)
*"What do you do?" "I'm a teacher. I work in a school."* (true all the time)

# 12

# Reality

## Reading and listening

**1** Read this true story about Glenna's experience with dreams and reality. Answer the questions. *media*

a) What ~~kind~~ of list did Glenna write? *dreams*
b) What kind of pictures did she put in a photo album?
*your life ~~magazine~~ and arranged*

# *Glenna's Dream Book*

One night I attended a seminar and heard a man speak. He explained that the mind thinks in pictures, not in words. He said that we can make our dreams become reality. We just have to follow six easy steps.

1 Make a list of the things that you want in your life.
2 Imagine pictures of the things that you want in your life.
3 Cut out pictures from magazines of the things on your list.
4 Put your pictures in a photo album.
5 Wait for your dreams to become reality.
6 Remember, there are no impossible dreams.

So I thought about what I wanted in life, and I wrote a dream list. After that, I cut up old magazines and arranged pictures of my dream list in a photo album. Then I sat back and waited.

## My dream list

1 I want to meet a good-looking man.
2 I'd like to have a traditional wedding.
3 I want to have flowers in my house every day.
4 I'd like to wear diamond jewelry.
5 I'd like to visit an island in the Caribbean.
6 I want to live in a beautiful new house.
7 I want to have a successful career.

**2** Read the story again. Match the things on Glenna's dream list with the pictures *a–g*.

**3** [cassette] 65 You are going to listen to more of Glenna's story. Did Glenna's dreams come true?

**4** Work with a partner. Listen again and mark each of the sentences true or false. Correct the false sentences.

T a) She met her future husband in California.
F b) She met him at work.
T c) He gave her roses every day.
T d) His hobby was collecting diamonds.
T e) They had a traditional wedding.
F f) They went to Hawaii for their honeymoon.
F g) They moved into a new house.
T h) Glenna told Jim about her dream book before they got married.
F i) She left her job.

**5** How many things from Glenna's dream list are on your dream list? Compare with a partner.

# Reality TV

**Vocabulary:**
**TV programs**

**1** 📼 66 You are going to listen to excerpts from eight different types of TV programs. Number the types of programs in the order in which you hear them.

| | |
|---|---|
| 1 | A game show |
| ☐ | A documentary |
| ☐ | The news |
| ☐ | A soap opera |
| ☐ | A sports program |
| ☐ | Reality TV |
| ☐ | A talk show |
| ☐ | The weather |

**2** What types of programs do you like/hate? Discuss with a partner.

**Writing**

**1** Work with a partner. Read the online application form below and discuss the questions.

a) What type of person do they want on *Big Brother*?

b) How much can you win?

c) In your opinion, which part of the form is the most difficult to fill in?

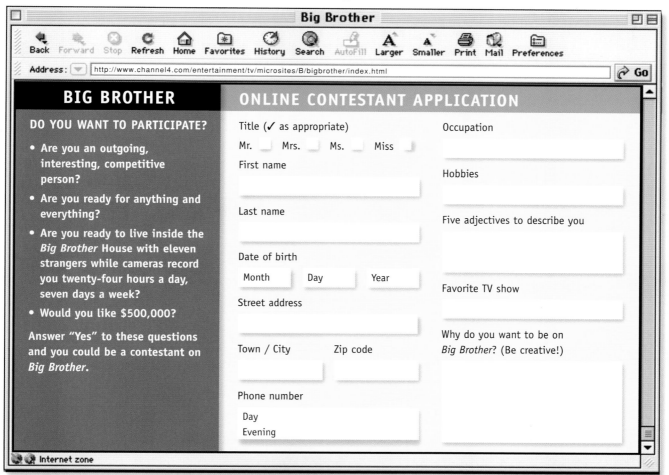

**2** Three people gave the following reasons for being on *Big Brother*. Who do you think the show's producers will choose? Discuss with a partner.

1 **Eric**: "I hope to win *Big Brother* and give the money to a friend who needs an expensive operation."

2 **Sheryl**: "I want to go on *Big Brother* because I'm really good-looking. The camera loves me!"

3 **Lynne**: "I'd like to meet new people and experience something new."

**3** Imagine you want to be on *Big Brother*. Fill in the form for yourself.

**4** Work as a class. Read each other's application forms. Vote for the best reason for being on *Big Brother*.

> **Big Brother**
>
> A group of adults live together in a house. TV cameras film them twenty-four hours a day. There are versions of *Big Brother* on TV all over the world.

# Close-up

**want to, 'd (would) like to, hope to**

Language Reference p. 53

**1** Rewrite the sentences so that they make sense.

a) I world travel to around want the *I want to travel around the world.*
b) married to I get want don't
c) lots like have of I'd to children
d) be to famous wouldn't I like
e) hope before fifty I I'm retire to

**2** Check (✓) the sentences that are true for you. Compare with a partner.

**3** Work in groups of three. Turn to page B90.

**(be) going to**

Language Reference p .53

Verb structures p. B99

**1** You are going to read and listen to an interview. Danielle, a TV personality, is talking to Lynne, the winner of *Big Brother*, about her plans for the future. Use the phrases in the box to complete the conversation. You can use the phrases more than once.

> I'm going to    I'm definitely not going to    you're going to    are you going to
> we're going to

D: Lynne, congratulations. How do you feel?
L: Oh, great. I feel fantastic. I'm so happy.
D: What's the first thing (1) *you're going to* do when you get out?
L: (2) _____ have a big party for all my friends. I missed them so much.
D: O.K. What (3) _____ do with the money?
L: Well, (4) _____ give some of it to charity, and with the rest, (5) _____ buy a house for my mom.
D: So, which of your *Big Brother* housemates (6) _____ see again?
L: There are some people I'd like to see again, and there are two people (7) _____ see again. I think you know who they are.
D: Yes, of course. That was really horrible. But your hair looks O.K. now.
L: Yeah, well…
D: Anyway Lynne, the question everyone wants to ask. You and Eddie became really good—uh—friends in the House. So (8) _____ see Eddie again?
L: Well, I don't know. Yes, of course (9) _____ see each other. But we don't know what's going to happen.
D: What advice would you give to future *Big Brother* contestants?
L: Don't do it! No, I'm just kidding. Be yourself, and be patient. It's very boring in there.
D: Finally, Lynne, what are your future plans?
L: Well, first (10) _____ go out and spend some money. Then I want to start my singing career. (11) _____ record a CD. Actually, I'd really like to be a television personality.
D: Oh—well, good luck.

**LANGUAGE TOOLBOX**

*(be) going to + verb*

I'm going to talk
You're going to talk
He's going to talk
She's going to talk
It's going to talk
We're going to talk
They're going to talk

**2** 📼 67 Listen and check your answers.

**3** Work with a partner. Each of these good intentions has one word missing. Rewrite each sentence with the word in the correct place.

a) I'm going get more exercise. (to) *I'm going to get more exercise.*
b) I going to save money. ('m)
c) I'm to spend more time with my family. (going)
d) I'm going plan my vacation earlier. (to)
e) I'm going to be late for appointments. (not)

**4** Which of the good intentions in 3 do you have? Discuss with a partner.

**5** Work with a partner. Student A: Turn to page B86. Student B: Turn to page B92.

# Language Reference: Future forms

**want to, 'd (would) like to, hope to**

We use these structures to talk about our dreams or desires for the future.

*We **want to** visit India next year.*

*One day, I'd **like to** climb Mount Fuji in Japan.*

*My sister **hopes to** go to college in England.*

**(be) going to**

We use (*be*) *going to* to talk about our future plans and intentions.

*I'm **going to** have a big party for all my friends.*

*We **aren't going to** stay for a long time.*

*Are you **going to** visit your parents this weekend?*

---

**Vowel sounds**

**1** Say the following words from the unit. In each group, (circle) the word with a different vowel sound from the other two.

a) game (dream) wait
b) mind type drink
c) <u>people</u> <u>reason</u> <u>island</u>
d) kind list think
e) ad<u>vice</u> bel<u>ie</u>ve onl<u>ine</u>
f) week make speak

**2** 🔲 **68** Listen, repeat the words, and check your answers to 1.

**3** Say the words in 1 again and add each one to an appropriate column in the chart.

| /i/ 6 words | /ɪ/ 3 words | /ai/ 6 words | /ei/ 3 words |
|---|---|---|---|
| *dream* | | | |

---

## I Have A Dream

**Song**

**1** 🔲 **69** Read and listen to the song. Choose the most appropriate word/phrase to complete the statements below. Compare your ideas with your partner.

a) It's a *positive / sad / romantic / ...*song.
b) I think the song is *great / O.K. / not bad / ... .*
c) I *often / sometimes / hardly ever / ...*listen to songs like this.

**Abba**

From Sweden, Abba was the most popular pop band in the world in the late 1970s and early 1980s.

**2** Complete these sentences with words from the song.

a) I had a bad d____ last night.
b) I have a particular song that I s____ when I'm happy.
c) I have to c____ with a lot of problems at my job.
d) When I was a child, I had a favorite fairy t____ .
e) I b____ in miracles.
f) I can see s____ good in everyone.

**3** Which sentences in 2 are true for you? Compare with a partner.

I have a dream, a song to sing,
To help me cope with anything.
If you see the wonder of a fairy tale
You can take the future even if you fail.
5  I believe in angels,
Something good in everything I see.
I believe in angels
When I know the time is right for me.
I'll cross the stream—I have a dream.

10  I have a dream, a fantasy
To help me through reality.
And my destination makes it worth the while,
Pushing through the darkness still another mile.
I believe in angels,
15  Something good in everything I see.
I believe in angels
When I know the time is right for me.
I'll cross the stream—I have a dream.
20  I'll cross the stream—I have a dream.

# 13 Things

## Reading

**1** Work with a partner and match pictures *a–j* with the words in the box.

> an address book    a cellphone    glasses    a glove    a handbag    keys
> money    a pet (snake)    a TV remote    a wedding ring

**2** The items in 1 are the top ten things people are most likely to lose. Which do you think are the top three things? Discuss with a partner. Then turn to page B90 and check your ideas.

**3** Work with a partner. Which three things do you think people are least likely to lose? Read the article and check your ideas.

## Lost and Found

The average person spends a year of his or her life looking for lost items.

Monday is the most common day to lose things.

In today's fast-moving society, we have more and more things to lose, more and more places to lose them, and less and less time to find them.

Research shows what men and women do when they lose things.

One in five women cry, and more than a quarter of men swear. Some women become violent.

The objects that people are least likely to lose are their car, passport, and laptop computer. Ninety-five to one hundred percent of people say they have never lost any of these items.

Of the things people wanted to lose, nearly half said "boring friends."

**4** Work in small groups. Refer to the *top ten things* in 2 and discuss the questions.

a) Which things do you have with you now/at home/at work or school?
b) Which things do you often lose/sometimes lose/never lose?
c) When was the last time you lost something? What happened?

## Listening

**1** 🔲 70 You are going to listen to a phone conversation between Judy and a clerk in an airport Lost and Found office. Judy lost a bag yesterday. Which bag did she lose (*a*, *b*, or *c*)?

**2** Complete the questions that the Lost and Found clerk asks in 1. Use the words in the box. Listen and check your answers.

> ~~What~~    How    Is there    What kind    Can    What's

a) *What* color is it?
b) what's it made of?
c) can you give me some more information?
d) How big is it?
e) Is there anything in it?
f) What kind of bag is it?

**3** Work with a partner. Turn to page B91.

**4** Work with a partner. Imagine you lost your own bag. Write a conversation between you and a Lost and Found clerk. Act out your conversation in front of the class.

# Shop Till You Drop

**1** Read the article about Karyn. Why did she set up the Web site *savekaryn.com*?

## savekaryn.com

**K**aryn lives in New York. Six months ago, she had a good job and she earned a good salary. But she didn't save her money. She spent it. In fact,
5 she had a big shopping habit and a credit card debt of $20,000.

There were the Gucci bags, the Prada shoes, and the La Prairie skincare products. She had a monthly hairdressing bill and a personal trainer.
10 She could afford it, but then she lost her job.

She soon found another job, but the salary was much lower…and she still had a credit card debt of $20,000.

She moved to a smaller apartment, bought
15 cheaper clothes and skincare products, and went out less…but she still had a huge credit card debt.

Then she had a brilliant idea. She started a Web site called *savekaryn.com* and put the following letter on it.

20 Hello everyone,
Thank you all for visiting my Web site! My name is Karyn. I'm really nice, and I'm asking for your help! The problem is that I have this huge credit card debt and I need $20,000 to pay it off. All I need is $1 from 20,000 people, or $2 from 10,000
25 people, or $5 from 4,000 people.
    SO I'M ASKING…
    Please help me pay off my debt. I am the girl at the office that MAKES YOU SMILE. Give me $1. Give me $5. Hell, give
30 me $20 if you feel like it! I promise that everything you give me will go toward paying off my debt.

    And they did. In fact, they sent her $13,323.08 in total, and in
35 just five months she was able to pay off her credit card debt. Now Karyn is an Internet celebrity, and she is looking forward
40 to helping others.

**2** Work with a partner. Discuss the questions.

- What kind of people do you think gave money to Karyn? *what person*
- When was the last time someday gave money to you?
- Who (or what) do you give money to? *whoever person*

**Vocabulary: money** **1** Complete each sentence with a word from the article in the previous section.

    a) I never *save* money. I always spend everything I earn. (line 4)
    b) I ____ too much money last weekend. (line 4)
    c) When I go shopping, I never pay cash; I always pay by ____ card. (line 6)
    d) My cellphone ____ is always huge. (line 9)
    e) I want a new stereo, but I can't ____ it. (line 10)

**2** Check (✓) the sentences in 1 that are true for you. Change the other sentences to make them all true for you. Compare your sentences with a partner.

**Anecdote** **1** 🔲 71 Think about the last time you went shopping. You are going to tell your partner about it. Read and listen to the questions and think about your answers.

☐ Where and when did you go shopping?          I went…
☐ What did you want to buy?                     I wanted to buy… (some CDs, a jacket, a camera, etc.)
☐ How long did you spend shopping?             I spent… (two hours, all day, the afternoon, etc.)
☐ Did you get what you wanted?                 Yes, I did. / No, I didn't.
☐ How much money did you spend?                I spent…
☐ How did you pay?                             I paid… (by credit card, by check, in cash, etc.)
☐ Did you enjoy your shopping trip?            Yes, I did. / No, I didn't.

**2** Think about what to say and how to say it. Use the sentence beginnings to help you.

**3** Tell your partner about the last time you went shopping.

**The schwa /ə/**

**1** [cassette icon] **72** Listen and repeat these chants. What do all the vowel sounds in red have in common?

| |
|---|
| I'm taller than my sister.<br>I'm taller than my brother.<br>I'm taller than my mother.<br>They're not as tall as me! |

| |
|---|
| I'm younger than my teacher.<br>I'm younger than my doctor.<br>I'm younger than my neighbor.<br>They're not as young as me! |

**2** Are any of the lines in the chants true for you? Use words from the box or your own ideas to make a chant that is true for you. Say your chant to the class.

| |
|---|
| short / shorter    old / older    fast / faster    slow / slower    rich / richer<br>poor / poorer    quiet / quieter    happy / happier    lucky / luckier |

# Close-up

**Comparatives**

( Language Reference p. 57 )

( Adjectives p. B100 )

**1** Work with a partner. The chart shows how to form comparative adjectives. Add one more adjective from the box to the appropriate column in the chart.

| |
|---|
| ~~rich~~    good    thin    interesting    friendly |

| + -er / r | double letter + -er | – y + -ier | irregular | more + adjective |
|---|---|---|---|---|
| nice → nicer<br>quiet → quieter<br>a) rich → richer | big → bigger<br>hot → hotter<br>b) ____ → ____ | curly → curlier<br>lucky → luckier<br>c) ____ → ____ | far → farther<br>bad → worse<br>d) ____ → ____ | generous → more generous<br>sensitive → more sensitive<br>e) ____ → ____ ____ |

*Things I'd like*

1  I'd like a richer boyfriend.
2  I'd like a more interesting job.
3  I'd like quieter weekends.

**2** Work with a partner. Combine comparative adjectives from 1 with nouns in the box—or your own ideas—and think about things you'd like.

| |
|---|
| a bedroom    a boyfriend    a car    a computer    a father    a girlfriend    hair<br>weekends    a house    a job    a mother    neighbors |

- Write two true sentences and one false sentence about things you'd like.
- Exchange sentences with your partner.
- Guess which of your partner's sentences is false. Discuss your ideas.

**3** Work with a partner. Complete each sentence with the correct form of the adjective.

a) I'm *taller* than Alex, but I'm not as *tall* as Ben. (tall)
b) I'm ____ than Carol but not as ____ as Denise. (old)
c) I'm ____ than Eddie but not as ____ as Frank. (relaxed)
d) My feet are ____ than Gina's but not as ____ as Heather's. (big)
e) My house is ____ from the school than Ian's but not as ____ as Jake's. (far)
f) My pen was ____ than Kerry's but not as ____ as Lisa's. (expensive)

**4** Replace the names in 3 with the names of people in the class to make the sentences true for you. Ask questions to check your information.

**Superlatives**

( Language Reference p. 57 )

( Adjectives p. B100 )

**1** Work with a partner. Write the comparative and superlative forms of the adjectives in the box.

| |
|---|
| ~~bad~~    ~~beautiful~~    busy    cheap    famous    far    good    modern    popular    ugly |

For example: *bad – worse than – the worst*
*beautiful – more beautiful than – the most beautiful*

**2** Work with a partner. Student A: Turn to page B87. Student B: Turn to page B93.

# Language Reference: Comparatives and superlatives

**All one-syllable and some two-syllable adjectives**
1 Adjectives ending in a consonant or "e."
  old—*older than*—the old**est**
  nice—*nicer than*—the nic**est**
2 Adjectives ending in a single vowel followed by a single consonant.
  big—*big**ger** than*—the big**gest**
3 Adjectives ending in "y."
  happy—*happ**ier** than*—the happ**iest**

**Irregular adjectives**
good—**better** *than*—the **best**
bad—**worse** *than*—the **worst**
far—**farther** *than*—the **farthest**

**Adjectives that have two or more syllables**
interesting—**more interesting** *than*—the **most interesting**
expensive—**more expensive** *than*—the **most expensive**

**Negative comparisons (*not as...as*)**
I'm **not as tall as** my father.

## The Most Valuable Things in the World

**Reading**

**1** Work with a partner. You are going to read an article about a dress that belonged to Marilyn Monroe. Guess the answers to the questions. Then read the article to check.

1 How tall was Marilyn Monroe?  a) 5 feet  b) 5 feet 5 inches  c) 6 feet
2 How old was she when she died?  a) 36  b) 42  c) 50
3 In what year did she wear the dress at John F. Kennedy's birthday celebration?
  a) 1955  b) 1962  c) 1968
4 How much did she pay for the dress?  a) $3,000  b) $7,000  c) $12,000
5 How much did a collector pay for the dress in 1999?
  a) $765,000  b) $942,000  c) $1,150,000

## *Happy Birthday, Mr. President...*

In May 1962, Marilyn Monroe sang "Happy Birthday, Mr. President" at John F. Kennedy's birthday celebration in New York.
5    She wore a skin-tight dress made of silk and covered in 6,000 beads. It cost her $12,000. Her hairdresser said, "Marilyn was amazingly beautiful that night, like a vision."
10    Thirty-seven years later, Christie's of New York held a "Personal Property of Marilyn Monroe" auction. Fifteen hundred items of Marilyn's property were sold, including the famous dress.

15    When Christie's looked for a model to wear the dress at the auction, they were surprised to find that the actress was only 5 feet 5 inches tall and very thin. "One of the smallest mannequins we found in the
20 United States was still not the correct size for the Happy Birthday dress," they said. "Marilyn was much smaller than people realized."
    When a collector bought the dress for $1,150,000, it became the most expensive
25 dress in the world. The buyer said that it was cheaper than he expected. He was prepared to pay $3,000,000. "I stole it," he said.
    There are few photos of Marilyn singing
30 "Happy Birthday, Mr. President," but it was her last memorable public performance. She died three months later at the age of 36.

**2** What is the most you usually pay for: a) a pair of sneakers; b) a pair of jeans; c) a dress or a pair of pants; d) a jacket or coat; e) a pair of shoes? Compare your answers with a partner.

**Vocabulary: large numbers**

Numbers p. 116

**1** 🎦 73 Say the numbers below. Then listen, check, and repeat.

a)  6 6 , 1 1 2  *Sixty-six thousand, one hundred twelve*
b)  1 9 4 , 4 5 9   c) 2 5 , 0 0 0   d) 1 5 7 , 9 4 7   e) 1 , 9 1 8 , 3 8 7   f) 3 2 4 , 1 8 8

**2** 🎦 74 The numbers in 1 were the highest prices ever paid in dollars for: *a bikini; a watch; a pair of jeans; a movie costume; some pop star clothing; a boxing robe.* Listen and match the items of clothing.

**3** What is the most valuable thing that you own? Discuss with a partner.

# Energy

## Reading

**1** You are going to read about Joaquín Cortés, a famous Spanish flamenco dancer. Complete the headings in the article.

| ~~Ancestry~~ | Eating | Family | Practice | Shoes | Sleep |
| Travel |

# Joaquín Cortés: *Body and Soul*

**1 *Ancestry***
His long dark hair is a symbol of his gypsy ancestry. He was born in 1969 in Córdoba, in southern Spain, and moved to Madrid when he was five.

**2** *Sleep*
He sleeps for five or six hours a night and wakes up full of energy.

**3** *Practice*
Cortés practices for more than five hours a day. His dance is so energetic that he loses 4 to 5 pounds during each performance.

**4** *Family*
He has a passion for women, but relationships are difficult because he is married to his work. His family is the most important thing to him—he sees them as often as possible.

**5** *Eating*
When he isn't performing, he eats three times a day. But when he is performing, he drinks coffee with milk all day and eats dinner late at night.

**6** *Travel*
Like a true gypsy, he travels all the time. But his means of transportation is not traditional—he travels by plane.

**7** *Shoes*
Cortés became interested in dance at the age of seven. His uncle, a flamenco dancer, was his hero. At the age of twelve, Cortés was part of a TV ballet troupe, and at fifteen he was a member of Spain's National Ballet company. Now, Cortés buys a new pair of flamenco shoes every month.

**2** The beginnings and the ends of these sentences are mixed up. Rewrite the sentences so that they are correct according to the article.

a) He sleeps *as often as possible.* → *He sleeps for five or six hours a night.*
b) He practices *every month.* He practices for more than 5 h. days
c) He sees his family *for five or six hours a night.* He sees them as often as possible
d) He eats *all the time.* He eats three times a day
e) He travels *for more than five hours a day.* He travels all the time
f) He buys new shoes *three times a day.* He buys new shoes pair of plamenco shoes every month

**3** Joaquín Cortés dances flamenco. Name five other styles of dance. Which is your favorite style? Discuss with a partner.

**/ʌ/ sound**

**1** Say the following words. In each group, circle the word with a different vowel sound from the other two.

a) come (home) son
b) front month score
c) morning color stomach
d) become other open
e) enough shoulder couple
f) shouldn't southern cousin

**2** ▭ 75 Listen, repeat the words, and check your answers to 1.

# Once or Twice?

**Vocabulary:**
**frequency expressions**

**1** Put the expressions (A–J) in the box in order of frequency on the line.

(A) once a month   (B) every ten years   (C) three times a day   (D) every year
(E) every two weeks   (F) twice a year   (G) once a day   (H) every four months
(I) twice a week   (J) four times a week

Not very frequent                                                           Very frequent

B                               A                               C

D                               G                               H
F  J                            E                               I

**2** Work with a partner. Follow the instructions.

- Point to the parts of the body referred to below (*This is my hair. These are my eyes*, etc.).
- Read the questions and write your answers. Use frequency expressions from 1.
- Ask your partner the questions and compare your answers.

**My hair:**     How often do you go to the hairdresser's?
**My eyes:**     How often do you sleep more than eight hours?
**My chest:**    How often do you exercise?
**My heart:**    How often do you fall in love?
**My stomach:**  How often do you eat?
**My legs:**     How often do you go dancing?
**My feet:**     How often do you go for a long walk?

**3** Work with a partner. Student A: Turn to page B87. Student B: Turn to page B93.

**Vocabulary:**
**parts of the body**

**1** Work with a partner. The words in the box are all parts of the body. Put each word into the correct column. Use your dictionary.

arm   back   finger   chin   ear   foot   hand   head   hip   knee   leg
lip   neck   nose   shoulder   stomach   toe   tooth   waist

| I have only one… | I have two… | I have… |
|---|---|---|
| back | arms | ten fingers |

**2** How flexible is your body? Write two things you can do and one thing you can't do with your body. Use the words in 1.

> 1  I can touch my left knee with my chin.
> 2  I can touch my left ear with my left shoulder.
> 3  I can't touch my nose with my right foot.

**3** Can your partner do the things you wrote down in 2? Ask your partner to demonstrate.

For example: *Can you touch your left knee with your chin?*

**Vocabulary:**
**combinations**

**1** Underline the correct word for each of these actions.

Stamp – timbre or sello

a) Bend your **knees** / head.          e) Clap your **hands** / knees.
b) Cross your **shoulders** / **legs**.     f) Stamp your legs / **feet**.
c) Fold your feet / **arms**.            g) Snap your head / **fingers**.
d) Nod your legs / **head**.            h) Shrug your **shoulders** / legs.

**2** 76 Listen, check your answers to 1, and do the actions. Work with a partner. Tell each other to do some of the actions.

# Image

**1** 🔊 **77** You are going to take a personality quiz. Listen and repeat the words in the box. <u>Underline</u> the stressed syllable. Which three adjectives best describe you? Compare with a partner.

> ad<u>ven</u>turous    charming    confident    energetic    exciting    impulsive
> interesting    loyal    pushy    quiet    selfish    serious    shy    unfriendly
> unsociable

**2** Take the quiz and compare the result with the words you chose to describe yourself in 1. Compare with a partner.

## HOW DO OTHER PEOPLE *Really* SEE YOU?

**1 When do you feel the best?**
 **a** In the morning.
 **b** In the afternoon and early evening.
 **c** Late at night.

**2 You usually walk...**
 **a** fast with long steps.
 **b** fast with short steps.
 **c** slowly with your head up.
 **d** very slowly.

**3 When you talk to people, you...**
 **a** stand with your arms folded.
 **b** have one or both hands on your hips.
 **c** have both your hands behind your back.
 **d** touch or push the person you are talking to.
 **e** play with your ear or touch your chin.

**4 When you relax, you sit with...**
 **a** your knees bent and your legs side by side.
 **b** your legs crossed.
 **c** your legs straight out in front of you.
 **d** one foot under you.

**5 Which of these colors do you like the most?**
 **a** Red or orange.       **e** Dark blue or purple.
 **b** Black.              **f** White.
 **c** Yellow or light blue.  **g** Brown or gray.
 **d** Green.

**6 In bed, you lie...**
 **a** on your back.        **d** with your head on one arm.
 **b** on your stomach.     **e** with your head under
 **c** on your side.            the covers.

### HOW TO SCORE

**1 a** 2  **b** 4  **c** 6

**2 a** 6  **b** 4  **c** 3  **d** 2

**3 a** 4  **b** 5  **c** 3  **d** 7  **e** 6

**4 a** 4  **b** 6  **c** 2  **d** 1

**5 a** 6  **b** 7  **c** 5  **d** 4  **e** 3  **f** 2  **g** 1

**6 a** 7  **b** 6  **c** 4  **d** 2  **e** 1

### WHAT YOUR SCORE MEANS

**36 or more:** People think you're confident, but also selfish and pushy. They admire you, but they don't enjoy your company.
**21–35:** People think you're exciting, impulsive, and adventurous. They love being in your company.
**16–20:** People think you're energetic and charming. You're always interesting.
**11–15:** People think you're unfriendly, but really you're just shy. You don't make friends easily, but you're very loyal.
**10 or less:** People think you're serious and unsociable. They think you are quiet and you prefer to spend time alone.

**3** Think about a member of your family or a friend for each description in *What Your Score Means* in the quiz. Tell your partner about the person.

# I'm Too Tired

Listening **1** Match the *Top Ten Excuses for Not Exercising* with the pictures (*a–j*).

1  "I'm too tired."
2  "I have a headache."
3  "I have too much work."
4  "I have a bad back."
5  "I have a stomachache."

6  "The swimming pool is too crowded."
7  "I have a cold."
8  "I don't have enough time."
9  "I don't have enough money."
10  "My foot hurts."

**2**  🔲 **78** Listen to a conversation between Danny and Louise. Check (✓) the excuses in 1 that Louise uses for not doing things.

**3**  Work with a partner. Make up conversations like the one in 2. Use your favorite excuses for not doing things.

## Close-up

**Problems and advice**

**1**  Complete each of these sentences with *too* or *enough*.

a)  My life is *too* busy.
b)  I have ____ much work.
c)  I have ____ many problems.

d)  I'm not relaxed ____ .
e)  I don't have ____ time.
f)  I don't have ____ money.

**2**  Are any of the sentences true for your partner? Find out.

> Verb structures p. B100

**3**  Put the words in the correct order to make sentences with *should/shouldn't*.

a)  Alex eats too much chocolate. (more  He  fruit  eat  should)
b)  Bella's computer isn't fast enough. (a  buy  She  one  should  new)
c)  Chris is too stressed out at work. (a  He  job  get  new  should)
d)  Dana doesn't get enough sleep. (stay  She  late  shouldn't  so  up)
e)  Ed drinks too much coffee. (should  He  water  more  drink)

**4**  Change the names in 3 to make true sentences about people you know.

## Language Reference: Problems and advice

**too** and **enough**
We use *too* before adjectives and *too many/much* before nouns.

    adjective               noun                    noun
*I'm **too** tired. I have **too much** work. There are **too many** problems.*

We use *enough* after adjectives and before nouns.

    adjective               noun                    noun
*It's not big **enough**. I don't have **enough** money. Do you have **enough** room?*

**should / shouldn't**
We can use *should* and *shouldn't* to give advice.
*You **should** get out more. You **should** be careful. You **shouldn't** work so late.*

# *Review 3*

## Looking Good

**Language reviewed**: frequency expressions, *How often...?* (Unit 14); future forms (Unit 12); comparatives and superlatives (Unit 13); physical description (Unit 11)

**Frequency expressions, *How often...?***

**1** Work with a partner. Arrange the frequency expressions in the box in the correct order (left to right) from *Not very frequent* to *Very frequent*.

> almost every day    twice a day    every nine days    twice a week
> at least once a week    every year

**2** Read this information about champion long-distance runner Paula Radcliffe. The underlined frequency expressions are all answers to questions. Write the questions.

For example: *Almost every day. – How often do you eat chocolate?*

# PAULA RADCLIFFE

What's life like for one of the UK's most famous female marathon runners?

**SPECIAL DIET**
She has to eat enough calories for her training program. She eats healthily, and she drinks about four quarts of water a day. But she's not obsessive—she eats chocolate underline(almost every day), and she has a glass of wine from time to time.

**TYPICAL TRAINING WEEK**
She works for eight days, and she runs underline(twice a day). She trains hard in the morning, with an easier session in the afternoon. Then underline(every nine days), she takes a day off.

**OTHER EXERCISE**
She works out at the gym underline(twice a week).

**AFTER TRAINING**
She sleeps for two hours every afternoon, and she tries to sleep ten hours a night. After training, she takes a cold bath or stands in a cold river or the sea for ten minutes. She gets a sports massage underline(at least once a week).

**VACATIONS**
She goes on vacation underline(every year) for three or four weeks and doesn't train at all. She likes water sports, relaxing on the beach, and dancing.

**3** Work with a partner. Ask each other the questions you wrote in 2.

For example: *"How often do you eat chocolate?" "Never."*

**Word stress** **1** Look at some of the words from Units 11–14. Say the words and add each one to an appropriate column in the chart. Underline the stressed syllable.

| A  ■. | B  ■.. | C  .■. |
|---|---|---|
| *camera* | *alcohol* | *appointments* |

> ~~alcohol~~   ~~appointments~~   ~~camera~~   collector   contestant   curly   earring
> exercise   favorite   generous   impulsive   island   lovely   neighbor
> performance   pushy   selfish   stomach   successful

**2**  79 Listen, check, and repeat the answers to 1.

**Future forms**

**1** Work with a partner. Complete the following sentences with *to*.

a) I want stay in and watch TV tonight.
b) I'm going buy some new clothes next weekend.
c) I want get a better cellphone—mine is very old.
d) I'd like join a gym and exercise more.
e) One day, I hope study at an American college.
f) I'd like learn another foreign language.

**2** Check (✓) the sentences in 1 that are true for you. Compare with a partner.

**3** Complete the sentences below so that they are true for you. Explain your sentences to a partner.

> **Eight ways to improve my life…**
> 1  I'm going to spend more time with…
> 2  I'm going to spend less time with…
> 3  I'm going to eat more…
> 4  I'm going to eat less…
> 5  I'm going to learn…
> 6  I'm going to travel to…
> 7  I'm going to…
> 8  I'm not going to…

**Comparatives and superlatives**

**1** Work in groups of three. Write the comparative and superlative forms for the adjectives in the box.

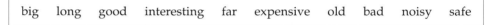

| big | long | good | interesting | far | expensive | old | bad | noisy | safe |

**My cellphone's bigger than yours.**

**2** Use the comparative forms of the adjectives in 1 or your own ideas to make three sentences about you and your two partners. Use the following sentence frame.

For example: *Eva's cellphone is older than Paulo's but not as old as Maria's.*

**3** Work in small groups. Answer the following questions.

a) Who is the best-looking man in the world?
b) Who is the best-looking woman in the world?
c) Who is the greatest actor of all time?
d) What is the most exciting sport to play or watch?
e) What is the most beautiful city in your country?
f) What is the worst program on TV now?

**4** Compare your answers to 3 with other groups. Vote on each of the questions.

**Anecdote**

**1** 🔲 80 Think about someone you think is good-looking. It can be someone you know or a famous person. You are going to tell your partner about him or her. Read and listen to the questions and think about your answers.

| ☐ What's his or her name? | His/Her name's… |
| ☐ What does he or she do? | He/She's… (a student, a designer, a model, etc.) |
| ☐ How old is he or she? | He/She's… |
| ☐ What color hair does he or she have? | He/She has… (blond hair, dark hair, a shaved head, etc.) |
| ☐ What style is it? | It's… (curly, long, straight, etc.) |
| ☐ What color eyes does he or she have? | He/She has… (big blue eyes, dark brown eyes, etc.) |
| ☐ What other features does he or she have? | He/She has… (a lovely smile, a diamond earring, etc.) |
| ☐ What kind of clothes does he or she wear? | He/She usually wears… (jeans, black tops, suits, etc.) |
| ☐ What do you think he or she is doing now? | He/She's probably… (studying, watching TV, etc.) |

**2** Think about what to say and how to say it. Use the sentence beginnings to help you.

**3** Tell your partner about this good-looking person.

# Clothes

**Language reviewed:** clothes (Unit 11); present continuous (Unit 11); *too* and *enough*, *should/shouldn't* (Unit 14)

**1** Work with a partner. Look at the scene in a women's clothing store. How many items of clothing in the box can you see in the picture?

| |
|---|
| belt   boots   coat   dress   earrings   jacket   jeans   pants pantyhose   ring   shirt   shoes   skirt   sneakers   socks suit   sunglasses   sweater   tie   T-shirt |

**2** Work with a partner. Put each word in the box in 1 in the appropriate column.

| I have a XXX. | I have a pair of XXX. |
|---|---|
| *belt* | *boots* |

**3** Work with a partner. Look at the different situations and discuss what you wear…

a) on the beach.
b) at a wedding.
c) at work or school.
d) when you go sightseeing.
e) at home on the weekend.
f) at a party.
g) when you work out.
h) in the country.
i) in bed.

**4** Work with a partner. The picture in 1 shows a scene from the skit on page 65. Richard and Ella are in a women's clothing store. Ella wants to buy a new dress, and the salesclerk is helping. Who do you think says the statements *a–h*? Write *R* for Richard, *E* for Ella, and *S* for the salesclerk.

a) I want to buy a new dress.
b) But you have at least fifty dresses.
c) Can I help you?
d) I'm just looking.
e) Can I try on this dress, please?
f) The fitting room is over there.
g) Do you have a larger size?
h) It looks good on you, ma'am. It's perfect.

**5** 81 Listen and read the skit on page 65. Check your answers to 4. Why does Richard say "OH, NOOOOO!" at the end?

**6** Work in groups of three. You are going to perform the skit.

a) Decide who is going to be Richard, who is going to be Ella, and who is going to be the salesclerk.
b) Practice your parts individually. Think about what voice your character has, what clothes he/she wears, and how he/she acts.
c) Perform the skit for the rest of the class.

# I Have Nothing to Wear

| | |
|---|---|
| **Scene** | A women's clothing store |
| **Characters** | Ella, Richard's wife |
| | Richard, Ella's husband |
| | Salesclerk |

5 *Richard and Ella are on the street, outside a woman's clothing store.*

| | | |
|---|---|---|
| **Richard** | *(Tired and unhappy)* | Where are we going now? |
| **Ella** | | I want to buy a new dress for Betty's party. |
| 10 | | |
| **Richard** | | But you have at least fifty dresses. |
| **Ella** | | Fifty?! Don't be silly. I have *nothing* to wear. Come on. |

*The clothing store door opens—music. Richard and* 15 *Ella go in.*

| | |
|---|---|
| **Salesclerk** | Can I help you? |
| **Ella** | No, thank you. I'm just looking. |
| **Salesclerk** | Are you looking for something for daytime or evening? |
| 20 **Ella** | Evening. I'm going to a party. |
| **Salesclerk** | The evening dresses are over there. |
| **Ella** | O.K., thanks… Hey, look at this dress, Richard. Do you like it? |
| **Richard** | *(Trying to show interest)* |
| 25 | Yes, yes. It's, uh, it's a nice, uh, color. |
| **Ella** | Excuse me. Can I try on this dress, please? |
| **Salesclerk** | Certainly. The fitting room's over there. |
| 30 **Ella** | Come on, Richard. |
| **Richard** | Yes, I'm here. |

*Musical interlude.*

| | |
|---|---|
| **Ella** | What do you think, Richard? |
| **Richard** | *(Too quickly)* |
| 35 | Yes, it's very nice. You should buy it. |
| **Ella** | I don't know. I think it's too small. Do you have a larger size? |

| | |
|---|---|
| **Salesclerk** | Not in that color. But I have a larger size in red. |
| 40 **Ella** | Red? I don't know. What do you think, Richard? |
| **Richard** | Uh, what? |
| **Ella** | A red dress. |
| **Richard** | Yes, fine. I like red. |
| 45 **Ella** | Can I try it on? |
| **Richard** | *(Groans)* |
| | Oh, no. I'm missing the football game. |
| **Ella** | Richard, this is important. |
| 50 **Salesclerk** | Here you are, ma'am. |
| **Ella** | Thank you. |

*Musical interlude.*

| | |
|---|---|
| **Ella** | What do you think? |
| **Salesclerk** | It looks good on you, ma'am. |
| 55 | It's perfect. |
| **Ella** | Richard? |
| **Richard** | *(Trying harder to show interest)* |
| | Yes, I love it. It's gorgeous. You look like a movie star. |
| 60 **Ella** | Do you think it's big enough? Isn't my stomach too fat? |
| **Richard** | Fat? What are you talking about? |
| **Ella** | So you really like it? |
| **Richard** | *(Impatient)* |
| 65 | Yes. |
| **Ella** | O.K., I'll take it. |
| **Richard** | Good. Can we go home now? |
| **Ella** | Well, I just want to get a pair of shoes. |
| **Richard** | Shoes?? You have at least a thousand |
| 70 | pairs of shoes. |
| **Ella** | Don't be silly. Come on… |
| **Richard** | OH, NOOOOO! |

# 16 *dotcom*

## Vocabulary: *to* + simple verb form

**1** Work with a partner. Match each Web site address with a reason for using it.

*Click here…*

a) www.cheapflights.com    1   to buy books.
b) www.yahoo.com    2   to buy and sell things.
c) www.flowers2send.com    3   to buy plane tickets.
d) www.eBay.com    4   to order flowers.
e) www.amazon.com    5   to get information about parties.
f) www.world-party.com    6   to search for information on the Internet.

**2** Which of the Web sites in 1 do you know or use? What other Web sites do you use? Why do you use them? Discuss with a partner.

For example: *I use www.cheapflights.com to find out flight times and to buy plane tickets.*

**3** Why do you use the following things? Choose two sentence beginnings and complete them in as many ways as you can. Compare your sentences with a partner.

a) I use my computer to _____ .      d) I use my credit card to _____ .
b) I use my cellphone to _____ .      e) I use my personal organizer to _____ .
c) I use my car to _____ .      f) I use my English to _____ .

For example: *I use my computer to send and receive e-mails, to find information,… etc.*

## Vocabulary: computer terms

**1** 🔊 82 Listen to the first conversation between Tom and his mom. What does Tom's mom want to do?

**2** Listen again and check (✓) the computer terms that Tom's mom understands. Put an ex (✗) by the terms she doesn't understand.

a) surf the Net ✓    d) desktop
b) send an e-mail    e) click
c) icon    f) mouse

**3** 🔊 83 Listen to the second conversation. <u>Underline</u> the computer terms in column A that Tom uses.

| A | | B | |
|---|---|---|---|
| a) | a file | 1 | to move information from the Internet to your computer. |
| b) | to search | 2 | to use your computer to look for information on the Internet. |
| c) | to go online | 3 | a flat surface on a computer where you see words and pictures. |
| d) | to save | 4 | to access a Web site—for example, by typing in a password. |
| e) | to download | 5 | a row of icons on a computer screen that perform actions when you click on them. |
| f) | a screen | 6 | to remove something from a computer. |
| g) | to delete | 7 | to connect to the Internet. |
| h) | a toolbar | 8 | a set of information such as a document or a picture that is stored on your computer. |
| i) | to log on | 9 | to make your computer retain information that you have put into it. |

**4** Work with a partner. Match the terms in column A in 3 with the definitions in column B. For example: *a) – 8.*

**5** Work in small groups. Write more English computer terms that are used in your language(s). Compare your lists. Which group has the longest list?

# dotcom Success

**Reading** **1** You're going to read an article about one of the most successful Web sites in Britain. Read the article quickly and discuss these questions with a partner.

a) What can you do if you log on to www.friendsreunited.com?
b) Why is www.friendsreunited.com so successful in Britain?
c) Do similar Web sites exist in your country?

# Where Are They Now?

**www.friendsreunited.com** is one of the most visited Web sites in Britain. Nearly ten million people log on to the site every day to find out what old friends are doing now.

5  Julie and Steve Pankhurst are the husband-and-wife team behind Friends Reunited. They met when they were both software engineers in the same company.

Julie had the original idea for the site in July 1999 when she was pregnant with her first child. She gave
10 up her job and set up the Web site as a hobby.

Friends Reunited now has millions of registered members. The company has spent nothing on advertising—they don't need the publicity, because everybody's talking about it. Word of mouth is their
15 best advertising.

"While the British are generally quite reserved," says Steve, "everyone wants to know what old classmates are doing."

The couple and their business partner have taken
20 on twelve employees who work from home. Most of them are mothers who Julie met in the hospital when she had her baby. Julie's sister works for the company, and a neighbor answers the e-mails.

The site has had many success stories—one man
25 was reunited with his mother after 53 years. Another was recently reunited with his cat after ten years. (His friend from college had looked after it.) Many childhood sweethearts
30 have been reunited and are now back together, some engaged to be married. The oldest member is a
35 99-year-old woman who is looking for old friends from school.

**2** Read the article more carefully and mark each sentence true or false. Correct the false sentences.

a) The person who had the original idea for the Web site was a pregnant woman.
b) His/Her previous job was as an accountant.
c) The Web site is advertised on television.
d) The Web site is popular because it helps people find old friends.
e) The offices are on a college campus.
f) The company employs 1,200 people.

**3** How many old friends from school do you still see now? Think about your elementary school, your high school, and your college. Compare with your partner.

**Vocabulary: phrasal verbs** **1** Complete the phrasal verb in each sentence with the correct particle (*after, on, out, up*).

a) I log *on* to the Internet at least once a day. (line 3)
b) I'd like to find _____ what my old classmates are doing now. (line 3)
c) I'm not going to give _____ my job when I have a baby. (lines 9–10)
d) I want to set _____ a Web site one day. (line 10)
e) I'd never take _____ family members in my own business. (lines 19–20)
f) I sometimes look _____ my neighbors' pet when they go on vacation. (line 28)

**2** Match the meaning of each phrasal verb in 1 with a word or expression in the box.

| create    take care of    access    hire    stop    discover |
| --- |

**3** Are any of the statements in 1 true for you? Compare with a partner.

**Reading** Work with a partner. Student A: Turn to page 92. Student B: Turn to page 104.

# Close-up

**Past participles**

Irregular verbs p. B102

**1** Copy and complete the verb chart with the three forms for each verb in the box. Which verbs have irregular forms?

| be | change | do | go | hear | make | meet | record | spend | travel | visit |

| Simple verb form | Simple past | Past participle |
| --- | --- | --- |
| *be* | *was, were* | *been* |
| *change* | *changed* | *changed* |

**2** 84 Darren and Nick meet up after getting back in touch through the Friends Reunited Web site. Use each past participle from 1 to complete their conversation. Listen, read, and check your answers.

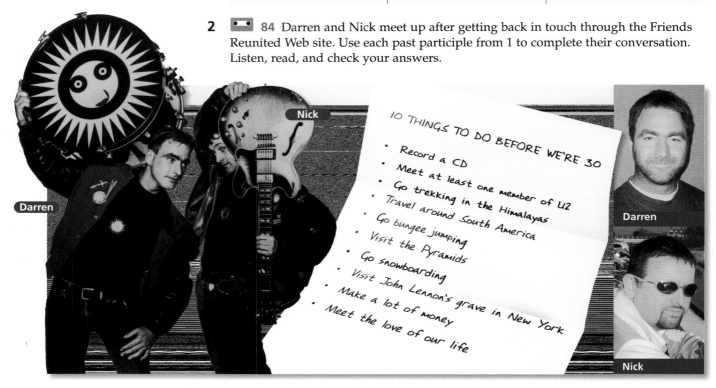

**10 THINGS TO DO BEFORE WE'RE 30**
- Record a CD
- Meet at least one member of U2
- Go trekking in the Himalayas
- Travel around South America
- Go bungee jumping
- Visit the Pyramids
- Go snowboarding
- Visit John Lennon's grave in New York
- Make a lot of money
- Meet the love of our life

Darren

Nick

**D:** Nick?

**N:** Darren! Wow, you haven't (1) *changed* at all.

**D:** And you look exactly the same—good to see you.

**N:** Wow, I can't believe it—after eleven years.

**D:** Yeah. Have you (2) _____ from any other friends from school?

**N:** Yes, a couple of people—that Friends Reunited Web site is great.

**D:** Hey, do you have that list?

**N:** Yes, here it is.

**D:** Oh yes, I remember—"10 things to do before we're 30." Well, we're 29—how many things have *you* (3) _____ ?

**N:** Not many—three, I think. I've been snowboarding, and I've gone bungee jumping, and I've (4) _____ John Lennon's grave in New York. And that's it, really. What about you?

**D:** Let's see—I haven't (5) _____ a CD—I stopped playing music when I finished school.

**N:** Yeah, me too.

**D:** And I've been to a U2 concert, but I haven't met any of them.

**N:** Have you (6) _____ much?

**D:** Well, I've (7) _____ to South America three times.

**N:** Wow.

**D:** But I haven't been to the Himalayas yet, or Egypt.

**N:** Have you ever gone snowboarding?

**D:** Yes, I've done that. But I haven't gone bungee jumping. I haven't (8) _____ a lot of money, either—I'm a teacher!

**N:** Ha ha. I've made a lot of money, but I've (9) _____ it. Anyway, have you met the love of your life?

**D:** No, I haven't (10) _____ anyone special yet. How about you?

**N:** Yes, I forgot to tell you. I'm married to Pamela.

**D:** Pamela?

**N:** Yes, you know, the gorgeous singer in our band.

**3** Work with a partner. Refer to the list "10 things to do before we're 30" and discuss.

a) Which things has Nick done?

b) Which things has Darren done?

c) Which things have you done?

**Present perfect**

Verb structures p. B99

*You haven't changed a bit.*

**1** Work with a partner. Complete the questions and write two possible answers.

a) *Have* you ever visited the Web site for your high school?  *Yes, I have.*  *No, I haven't.*
b) *Has* your school ever tried to get in touch with you?  *Yes, it _____ . No, it _____ .*
c) _____ you ever gone to a high school reunion?  _____  _____
d) _____ you ever gotten an e-mail from an old friend?  _____  _____
e) _____ your parents ever sent you an e-mail?  _____  _____
f) _____ you ever met somebody new on the Internet?  _____  _____

**2**  85 Listen, check, and repeat. Work with a partner. Ask and answer the questions in 1. Discuss your answers.

**3** The questions and answers in 1 refer to completed actions in time up to and including now. What is the name of the tense used? How do you form the affirmative, negative, and question forms of this tense?

**4** Work with a partner. Student A: Turn to page B88. Student B: Turn to page B94.

## Language Reference: Present perfect

We can use the present perfect to describe completed actions that have taken place in time up to and including now.
We often use *ever* to mean "in your life."

*"**Have** you **ever met** somebody on the Internet?" "Yes, I have./No, I haven't."*
*"**Has** your teacher **ever spoken** to you in Chinese?" "Yes, he has./No, he hasn't."*

Note: The past participle of *go* is *gone*. However, when we refer to some activities, we can use *been* instead of *gone*.

*"I went skiing last year, but I've never been/gone snowboarding." "I've never been/gone skiing."*

Also, when we refer to visiting a place, we use *been* instead of *gone*.

*"Did you go to New York last year?"*
*"No, I didn't. I've never been to New York."*

Note: We cannot use the present perfect to describe *when* a completed action took place. We must use the simple past.

*I went to New York three years ago.*
NOT ~~I've been to New York three years ago.~~

*He met the love of his life in 1996.*
NOT ~~He's met the love of his life in 1996.~~

**Time up to and including now**

↑  ↑  ↑  ↑  ↑

*I've been to New York many times.*

---

**Anecdote**

**1**  86 Think about an old friend you would like to get in touch with. You are going to tell your partner about him or her. Read and listen to the questions and think about your answers.

☐ What's his or her name?  His/Her name's…
☐ Where did you first meet?  We first met… (at school, at the gym, etc.)
☐ How old were you?  I… (was 13, can't remember, etc.)
☐ Why did you become friends?  Because… (we liked the same music, etc.)
☐ What kinds of things did you talk about?  We talked about… (boyfriends, girlfriends, etc.)
☐ What kinds of things did you do together?  We… (went shopping, went out, etc.)
☐ What is your best memory of him or her?  My best memory is… (our vacation in…, etc.)
☐ When was the last time you saw him or her?  The last time I saw him/her was… (in 1997, etc.)
☐ Why would you like to get in touch with him or her?  I'd like to get in touch because… (I always liked him/her, he/she had a great sense of humor, etc.)

**2** Think about what to say and how to say it. Use the sentence beginnings to help you.

**3** Tell your partner about this old friend.

# 17 Drive

### Reading

**1** Work with a partner. You are going to read an article about the best and the worst drives to work. Read these sentences. Write *B* if you think it refers to the best drive and *W* if you think it refers to the worst drive.

a) Jack believes that his drive to work is the most spectacular drive in the world. *B*
b) Her office is four miles from her house, but it takes two hours to get there.
c) Every morning, he drives to work along the coast.
d) Traffic moves along Sukhumvit Road downtown at a third of a mile an hour.
e) "Now, everybody has a car, and there aren't enough roads in the city."
f) As he drives through the National Park, he often sees koalas.

**2** Read the article and check your answers. Which drive is similar to your drive to work/school? Tell your partner.

# Driving to Work

## THE BEST DRIVE

**JACK SPENCER** has an unusual job. He's a lighthouse tour guide. Cape Otway lighthouse is situated near the Great Ocean Road, about 125 miles from Melbourne in southern Australia.

Jack believes that his drive to work is the most spectacular drive in the world.

"Hundreds of thousands of tourists come to Victoria every year to drive along the Great Ocean Road and see the amazing scenery. I do it every day on my way to work," he says. Jack lives in Portland, about 30 miles from Cape Otway.

Every morning, he drives to work along the coast. It takes him about forty minutes. "Traffic isn't a problem," Jack says. "I'm usually on the road before the tourists get up."

He drives past dramatic rock formations like the Twelve Apostles, through rainforests, and past spectacular waterfalls. As he drives through the National Park, he often sees koalas.

"From the top of my lighthouse, I have the best view in the world," says Jack.

## THE WORST DRIVE

**SIRIWAN** lives in the Thai capital, Bangkok, with her husband and two children.

Her office is four miles from her house, but it takes her two hours to get there by car in the morning.

"Some cities have problems with crime, taxes, bad weather — here we have traffic jams," says Siriwan.

Before she goes to the office, she has to take her children to school — so she starts out from her house at 5 A.M. The children sleep until they arrive at school. Then Siriwan wakes them up and gives them breakfast in the car. The children go into school, and Siriwan begins her trip to the office.

In the evening, the traffic is even worse. Traffic moves along Sukhumvit Road downtown at a third of a mile an hour. In the rainy season, it doesn't move at all.

But why is it so bad? "In the past, more people moved around Bangkok by boat. Now, everybody has a car, and there aren't enough roads in the city. The new skytrain has helped a little, but right now, it has only two lines."

# Close-up

Questions with
*How* + adverb/adjective
and *What* + noun

**1** Work with a partner. Complete the comprehension questions for the article on page 70 with words from the box.

| ~~far~~ | far | fast | kinds | long | long | many | often | time |
|---|---|---|---|---|---|---|---|---|

a)  How *far* is it from Cape Otway to Melbourne?

b)  How _____ tourists come to Victoria every year?

c)  How _____ does Jack drive along the Great Ocean Road?

d)  How _____ does it take Jack to drive to work?

e)  What _____ of scenery does Jack drive through?

f)  How _____ is it from Siriwan's house to her office?

g)  How _____ does it take Siriwan to get to her office?

h)  What _____ does Siriwan start out from her house?

i)  How _____ does the traffic move along Sukhumvit Road in the evening?

**2** Read the article on page 70 again and answer the questions in 1.

**3** Work with a partner. Student A: Turn to page B89. Student B: Turn to page B95.

## Language Reference: Question forms

**Questions with *How* + adverb/adjective and *What* + noun**

We can form many different questions by combining *How* + adverb/adjective (*How...far, many, often, tall*, etc.) and *What* + noun (*What...color, size, kind, time*, etc.).

| question word | auxiliary | subject | |
|---|---|---|---|
| *What color* | *are* | *your eyes?* | |
| *What time* | *do* | *you* | *get up?* |
| *How many people* | *can* | *you* | *fit in your car?* |
| *How long* | *does* | *it* | *take you to get to work?* |
| *How far* | *is* | *your job* | *from your house?* |

Vocabulary:
prepositions of
movement

**1** Work with a partner. Choose the correct alternative to complete each of these sentences.

On my way to work…

a)  I go **down / through** the stairs.

b)  I go **out of / along** my apartment.

c)  I go **through / across** the street.

d)  I go **through / along** the park.

e)  I go **into / along** the river.

f)  I go **up / over** a bridge.

g)  I go **across / up** a hill.

h)  I go **past / down** some stores.

i)  I go **into / down** my office.

**2** Think about your own way to work or school. How many of the sentences in 1 are true for you? Compare with a partner.

**3** Write a description of your way to work or school. Try to use each preposition in 1 at least once. Reorder the sentences and change the underlined words as necessary. Compare your description with a partner's.

**LANGUAGE TOOLBOX**

past

through

over

along

across

up

down

into

out of

# It Drives Me Crazy!

**Listening**    **1**   ⊡ 87 You are going to listen to six people talking about what drives them crazy on the road. Listen and match the people (1–6) to the pictures (a–f).

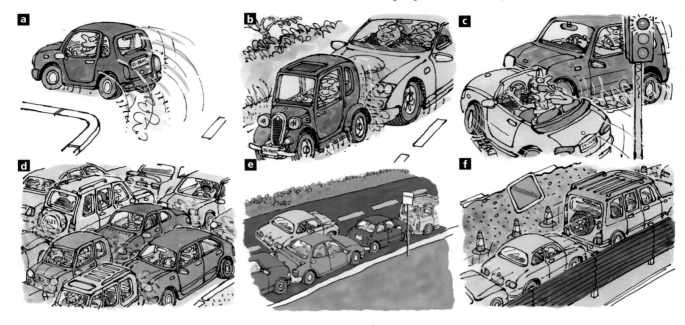

**2**   Work with a partner. Complete the following task.

- Match key words and expressions in the box with the pictures in 1.
  For example: *a) – signal …*
- Think of three situations that drive you crazy on the road. Use the situations in 1 or your own ideas.
- Tell your partner. Begin: *"I can't stand it when…"*

> impossible to pass    double-park    ~~signal~~    turn left    turn right
> go straight    get stuck in traffic    rush hour    construction
> take the highway    have an accident    the traffic lights

**Ordinal numbers**    **1**   ⊡ 88 Work with a partner. Complete the following chart. Listen and repeat the ordinal numbers.

| 1st | 2nd | 3rd | 4th | | 6th | 7th | | 9th | |
|-----|-----|-----|-----|-----|-----|-----|-----|-----|-----|
| *first* | | | | *fifth* | | | *eighth* | | *tenth* |

**2**   ⊡ 89 Look at the street map. Listen to three sets of directions from A to B. Match starting points A1, A2, A3 with finishing points B1, B2, B3.

1   A1 → _____
2   A2 → _____
3   A3 → _____

**3**   Work with a partner. Use the map and take turns giving directions from A to B. Then think about the area around your school. Take turns giving similar directions to stores, bars, restaurants, etc. near the school.

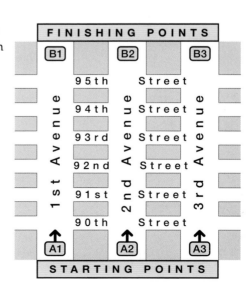

# On the Way Home

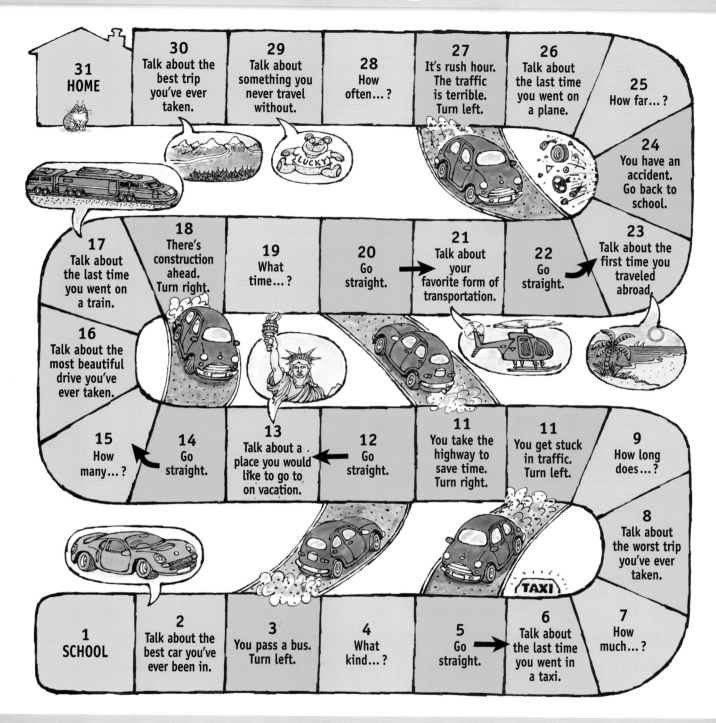

**31 HOME**

**30** Talk about the best trip you've ever taken.

**29** Talk about something you never travel without.

**28** How often...?

**27** It's rush hour. The traffic is terrible. Turn left.

**26** Talk about the last time you went on a plane.

**25** How far...?

**24** You have an accident. Go back to school.

**17** Talk about the last time you went on a train.

**18** There's construction ahead. Turn right.

**19** What time...?

**20** Go straight.

**21** Talk about your favorite form of transportation.

**22** Go straight.

**23** Talk about the first time you traveled abroad.

**16** Talk about the most beautiful drive you've ever taken.

**15** How many...?

**14** Go straight.

**13** Talk about a place you would like to go to on vacation.

**12** Go straight.

**11** You take the highway to save time. Turn right.

**11** You get stuck in traffic. Turn left.

**9** How long does...?

**8** Talk about the worst trip you've ever taken.

**1 SCHOOL**

**2** Talk about the best car you've ever been in.

**3** You pass a bus. Turn left.

**4** What kind...?

**5** Go straight.

**6** Talk about the last time you went in a taxi.

**7** How much...?

## HOW TO PLAY

Play the game in small groups. You will need a die and counters.

1   Place your counters on the square marked SCHOOL and throw the die.

2   The first player to throw a six starts the game.

3   The first player throws the die and moves his/her counter along the road according to the number on the die.

4   Players then take turns moving along the road.

5   When a player lands on a green square, he/she has to talk about the subject for 30 seconds.

6   When a player lands on a blue square, each of the other players asks him/her a question beginning with the question word. If a player has nothing to say, he/she is allowed to pass and miss a turn.

7   When a player lands on a red square, he/she has to follow the instructions.

8   The game continues until the first player reaches the square marked HOME.

# Justice

### Reading

1   You are going to read two stories. The six pictures below (*a–f*) are important in the stories. Complete the labels with the words in the box.

> ~~paint~~   bag   wine   club   scissors   party

a) a can of <u>paint</u>   b) a dinner ____   c) a night____   d) a bottle of ____   e) a plastic ____   f) a pair of ____

2   Read the stories and match items *a–f* in 1 to the appropriate story. What is the importance of each item in the stories? Tell your partner.

## Revenge Is Sweet

When Lady Sally Moon found out that her husband was having an affair, she didn't leave him. She thought it was better to be unhappily married than not married at all. But her husband
5   didn't hide his affair, and this made her feel really bad.
    One day she was driving home when she saw his car parked outside his lover's house. She was angry, and she decided to get her revenge. She
10   quickly drove home, put a can of paint into her car, and drove to the lover's house.
    Then she poured thick white paint all over her husband's beautiful new black car.
    Next, she carefully took his collection of fine
15   wines from the cellar. That night she went around the village where she lived and quietly placed a bottle of wine on each doorstep. She left the other bottles on the war memorial in the center of the village.
20   Finally, she took a pair of scissors and cut off the arms and legs of all his suits—38 of them in all.

## Meal Mail

Last year, I went out with Cindy for four months. We were very different. I was always early; she was always late. I was very neat; she was very messy. But to be honest, I found the differences
5   rather attractive.
    At first, she was only fifteen or twenty minutes late. But she got later and later.
    At the end of August, it was my birthday. I'm a good cook, so I decided to have a dinner party,
10   and I invited four friends.
    That evening, my four friends arrived on time, but not surprisingly Cindy wasn't there at eight o'clock. But then she wasn't there at nine o'clock, nine-thirty or ten o'clock.
15   This was extremely late, even for Cindy. So I called her cellphone. When she answered, music was playing loudly in the background. "Where are you?" I shouted angrily. "I'm at a nightclub," she shouted back. I was furious. I went into the
20   kitchen and put her dinner in a plastic bag.
    The next morning I mailed it to her with a note saying, "Here's your dinner." A week later I got a postcard from Cindy. It said, "Too much salt."

3   ▶️ 90 Work with a partner. Choose the correct ending for each story. Read and listen and check your answers.

   a)   The following week, I have another dinner party.
   b)   As you can imagine, I never saw her again.
   c)   Her husband wasn't very happy when he got home.
   d)   In the end, I apologized to my friends.
   e)   After that, she felt much better.
   f)   A few days later, she went skiing.

4   Which story do you like better? Tell your partner why.

**Vocabulary:
time adverbials**

**1** Read the stories on page 74 again. Write the time adverbials in the box in the order in which they appear in the stories.

<del>One day</del>  <del>Last year</del>  At first  Then  At the end of August  Next
That night  That evening  The next morning  Finally  A week later

**Revenge Is Sweet**
a) *One day*
b) ____
c) ____
d) ____
e) ____

**Meal Mail**
1 *Last year*
2 ____
3 ____
4 ____
5 ____
6 ____

**2** Work with a partner. Choose a story. Take turns using the time adverbials in 1 to retell the story *without* looking at the text on page 74.

**Vocabulary:
adverbs of manner**

**1** Work with a partner. Complete the charts with adverbs and adjectives from the stories on page 74.

*Revenge Is Sweet*

| Adjective | | Adverb |
|---|---|---|
| a) unhappy | | *unhappily* |
| b) ____ | | badly |
| c) ____ | | angrily |
| d) quick | | ____ |
| e) ____ | | beautifully |
| f) careful | | ____ |
| g) quiet | | ____ |

*Meal Mail*

| Adjective | | Adverb |
|---|---|---|
| 1 *different* | | differently |
| 2 early | | ____ |
| 3 late | | ____ |
| 4 ____ | | neatly |
| 5 ____ | | attractively |
| 6 ____ | | well |
| 7 loud | | ____ |

**2** Work with a partner. Use the information in the charts in 1 to answer the questions on adverb formation.

   a) How do you make adverbs from most adjectives?
   b) How do you make adverbs from adjectives ending in *y*?
   c) What are the adverbs for the adjectives *good, early, late*?

**3** Rewrite these sentences in the usual order.

                      subject + verb + object  +  adverb
   a) I slowly eat very food my      *I*   *eat*   *my food*   *very slowly.*
   b) I very drive car quickly my
   c) I days plan my carefully very
   d) I play badly guitar the very
   e) I my money spend very intelligently
   f) I for arrive very appointments early
   g) I phone talk the on very quietly
   h) I speak very well English

**4** How many sentences in 3 are true for you? Rewrite the sentences so that they are all true for you. Compare your sentences with a partner.

## Punctuation

**LANGUAGE TOOLBOX**

| ABC | capital letters |
|-----|-----------------|
| abc | lowercase letters |
| . | period |
| ? | question mark |
| ! | exclamation point |
| , | comma |
| – | dash |
| ' | apostrophe |
| " " | quotation marks |

**1** Work with a partner. Rewrite the story with the correct punctuation and capital letters.

> a shoplifter was trying to steal a watch from an exclusive jewelry store when the manager caught him
>
> please dont call the police Ill buy the watch said the shoplifter
>
> the manager thought about it for a minute and then said well all right thats 500 dollars
>
> oh dear said the shoplifter thats more than I planned to spend can you show me something less expensive

**2** Work with a partner. You are going to read another story, called *Usher's Revenge*. Look at the pictures and follow the instructions.

- Find out the meaning of each expression in the box. Use a dictionary.
- Discuss what you think happens in the story.
- Student A: Turn to page B89. Student B: Turn to page B95.

| mystery play   stage   usher   tip   front row   whisper |
|---|

# Close-up

## Past continuous

Language Reference p. 77

Verb structures p. B99

**1** Work with a partner. Look at this sentence from the story *Revenge Is Sweet* on page 74. Discuss the questions.

*One day she <u>was driving</u> home when she <u>saw</u> his car parked outside his lover's house.*

a) Which <u>underlined</u> verb is in the simple past tense? Which <u>underlined</u> verb is in the past continuous tense?

b) Which tense do you use to describe something that was in progress when another event happened?

c) Which tense do you use to describe an event that happened at a particular moment?

**2** Work with a partner. Complete the questions and write two possible answers.

| | | | |
|---|---|---|---|
| a) | *Were* you living in the same house this time last year? | Yes, I was. | No, I wasn't. |
| b) | *Were* your parents watching TV at 11:30 last night? | Yes, they ____ | No, they ____ |
| c) | ____ you studying in your English class this time yesterday? | ____ | ____ |
| d) | ____ it raining when you woke up this morning? | ____ | ____ |
| e) | ____ you wearing a hat when you went out this morning? | ____ | ____ |
| f) | ____ you speaking English when the class started? | ____ | ____ |

**3** 🔊 91 Listen, check, and repeat. Work with a partner. Ask and answer the questions in 2. Discuss your answers.

# Language Reference: Past continuous

We often use the past continuous in stories. We can use it to describe something that was in progress when another event happened.

He **was working** in a bookstore when he first met Sandra.
They **were watching** their favorite TV show when the doorbell rang.
I **was sleeping** when you called me.

# Once Upon a Time

**Writing a story**

**1** Work with a partner. The pictures illustrate a modern fairy tale. Match the words in the box to the appropriate pictures and discuss what the story is about.

> a frog    a castle    children    a beautiful princess    an evil witch
> a handsome prince    a kiss    a pond    clothes

**2** Work in groups of three to five. You are going to write the story. Discuss answers to the questions in column A, and discuss ways of completing the sentence beginnings in column B. Give your story a title.

Have you ever heard the story of the princess and the frog?
Well, once upon a time, there was a princess. ...

| A | B |
|---|---|
| a) What kind of person was the princess? | She was... |
| b) Where did she live? | She lived in... |
| c) Where was she sitting? | One day, she was sitting... |
| d) What was she thinking about? | She was thinking about... |
| e) Who did she meet? | There she met... |
| f) What did he say to her? | He said to her,... |
| g) What happened later? | Later,... |

**3** 📼 92 Listen to the original story and compare it with your own. What are the differences?

**4** Listen again to the original story and answer the questions in column A in 2.

**5** Work with the class. Compare stories and decide which ending is the best one.

# 19 Extreme

**Reading** **1** You are going to read and listen to a poem. Before you read the poem, match each of the word lists *A–D* to the photographs *1–4*. Find the meaning of each word. Use your dictionary if necessary. For example: *A–3*.

| A | B | C | D |
|---|---|---|---|
| fields | a <u>de</u>sert | snow | a vol<u>ca</u>no |
| a <u>ri</u>ver | stars | ice | a sea |
| clouds | <u>pla</u>nets | a <u>gla</u>cier | cliffs |
| a <u>rain</u>bow | space | | |

**2** ▭ **93** Read and listen to the poem. What do you think the correct title is?

a) *I Hate Geography*
b) *I Love Geography*
c) *I Don't Mind Geography*

**3** Work with a partner. Which geographical features in the pictures in 1 can you see in your country? Where?

**Word and sentence stress** **1** The poem above has a very regular stress pattern. <u>Underline</u> the stressed syllables on each line.

**2** ▭ **94** Listen and repeat the poem at the same time as the recording. Keep in time with the beat.

**3** ▭ **95** Listen and say the poem in time with the beat.

*I ___ Geography*

<u>Other people</u>, <u>other places</u>,
<u>Different customs</u>, <u>different faces</u>,
Drought and desert, field and plain,
Snow and ice and monsoon rain,
Volcanoes, glaciers,
Bubbling springs,
Clouds and rainbows,
Countless things.
Stars and planets, distant space,
Whatever's ugly, full of grace.
Seas and rivers,
Cliffs and caves,
The wondrous ways this world behaves.
So much to learn; so much to know;
And so much farther still to go.

**by John Kitching**

# Extreme Hotels

**1** Work with a partner. You are going to read an article about a hotel in Sweden. Match the figures in column A with the probable meanings in column B. Then read the article and check your answers.

| A | B |
|---|---|
| 40,000 | = Year the first hotel was constructed. |
| 1990 | = Temperature in Fahrenheit inside the hotel. |
| 64 | = Tons of ice and snow used to build the hotel. |
| 14,000 | = Temperature in Fahrenheit outside the hotel. |
| -22 | = Number of rooms in the hotel. |
| 23 | = Number of hotel guests last year. |

# THE COOLEST HOTEL IN THE WORLD

5  Can you imagine a hotel that is made entirely of ice? Well, it exists in Sweden, but only in the winter. In the spring, the hotel melts away and disappears into the river.

The Ice Hotel is situated on the shores of the Torne River in the old village of Jukkasjarvi, Sweden.

Every winter, work starts on building a new Ice Hotel, involving 40,000 tons of ice and snow.
10  10,000 tons of ice is taken from the Torne River, and 30,000 tons of snow is provided by Mother Nature.

The first Ice Hotel was constructed in 1990. It started as a single room—now it has 64 rooms, as
15  well as an Ice Chapel, an art gallery, a theater, a movie theater, and an Absolut Ice Bar. Last winter, more than 14,000 guests spent the night at the Ice Hotel.

Outside, the temperature is -22°F, but inside the
20  hotel, the temperature is always around 23°F. All the furniture is made of ice, including the beds, but nobody gets cold. The beds are covered with reindeer skins, and guests are given warm clothes and special arctic sleeping bags.
25  In the Absolut Ice Bar, the drinks are served in glasses made of ice, so there is no need for ice cubes!

Every year, the interior of the hotel is designed by different artists from all over the world. It is
30  described by visitors as "absolutely stunning," "one of the most beautiful places I've ever seen," and "unique."

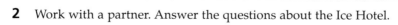

**2** Work with a partner. Answer the questions about the Ice Hotel.

a) Where is it situated?
b) What is it made of?
c) What is the furniture made of?

d) What are the beds covered with?
e) Who is the interior designed by?
f) How is it described by visitors?

**3** Answer the questions in 2 for a building you know well. Tell your partner about the building.

For example: *The Empire State Building is in New York. It's made of steel and...*

# Close-up

**Passives**  **1**  Work with a partner. Look at the active and passive sentences below and answer the questions.

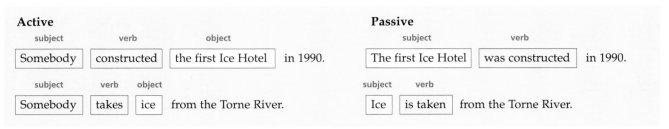

| Active | | |
| --- | --- | --- |
| subject | verb | object |
| Somebody | constructed | the first Ice Hotel | in 1990. |

| subject | verb | object |
| --- | --- | --- |
| Somebody | takes | ice | from the Torne River. |

| Passive | |
| --- | --- |
| subject | verb |
| The first Ice Hotel | was constructed | in 1990. |

| subject | verb |
| --- | --- |
| Ice | is taken | from the Torne River. |

a) Find the objects of the active sentences. Are they: (1) before the verb; (2) after the verb?

b) Find the same words in the passive sentences? Are they: (1) before the verb; (2) after the verb?

c) True or false? The object of an active sentence becomes the subject of a passive sentence.

d) Look at the first word of the verb in the passive sentences. Is it a form of: (1) *be*; (2) *do*; (3) *have*?

e) Look at the second word. Is it: (1) the simple form; (2) the simple past form; (3) the past participle?

f) True or false? Passive verbs consist of a form of *be* plus a past participle.

g) Read all the sentences. Does *somebody* appear in the active or the passive sentences?

h) Do we know who *somebody* is?

i) True or false? We can use the passive to talk about actions when we don't know who performed them.

**2**  Work with a partner. Complete the questions and write two possible answers.

a) *Was* your house built before 1980?  Yes, it *was*.  No, it *wasn't*.
b) *Were* your shoes designed in Italy?  Yes, they ___  No, they ___
c) *Is* your salary paid by check?  Yes, ___  No, ___
d) ___ you invited to any parties last week?  ___  ___
e) ___ your name spelled the same way in English? ___  ___
f) ___ your cellphone made in Japan?  ___  ___

**3**  [cassette] 96 Listen, check, and repeat. Work with a partner. Ask and answer the questions in 2. Discuss your answers.

## Language Reference: Passives

In passive sentences, the object of the active verb becomes the subject of the passive verb.

| Active | | |
| --- | --- | --- |
| subject | verb | object |
| Somebody | constructed | the first Ice Hotel | in 1990. |

| Passive | |
| --- | --- |
| subject | verb |
| The first Ice Hotel | was constructed | in 1990. |

The passive is formed with *be* (*am, is, are, was, were*) + past participle (*constructed, taken*, etc.—see *Irregular Verbs* on page B102). We can use the passive to talk about actions when we don't know who performed them or when it is not important to know who performed them.

*My shoes **were designed** in Italy.  My house **was built** before 1980.  The beds **are covered** in reindeer skins. All the furniture **is made** of ice.  My salary **is paid** by check.*

# What's the Weather Like?

**Vocabulary: the weather**

**1** Complete the chart with appropriate words.

| | ☀ | ☁☁☁ | ☁☁ | 〰〰 | 〰➡ | ❄❄❄ | ⛈⚡⛈ |
|---|---|---|---|---|---|---|---|
| **Noun** | (1) *sun* | cloud | (3) ____ | fog | (5) ____ | snow | (7) ____ |
| **Adjective/ Phrase** | It's sunny. It's nice/dry. It's warm/ hot. | It's (2) ____. It's overcast. | It's rainy/wet. It's raining. | It's (4) ____. | It's windy. | It's (6) ____. It's snowing. It's cold/ freezing. | It's stormy. |

**2** Read the winter weather forecast for the North Pole. Would you like to go there? Tell your partner.

## THE NORTH POLE IN THE WINTER

Today will start off with <u>extremely cold</u> temperatures of <u>minus 22</u> degrees Fahrenheit. It will be <u>very windy</u> in the afternoon, and there will probably be <u>a snowstorm</u> later on. It will be <u>dark</u> all day. Tomorrow will be the same, and the next day, and the day after. Next week might be a little <u>warmer</u>, but not much.

**3** 🔲 97 Work with a partner. Invent a winter weather forecast for New York by replacing the <u>underlined</u> words and phrases in 2. Listen and compare your ideas.

**Vocabulary: *will* and *might***

Verb structures p. B100

**1** Complete these predictions about the weather.

**will happen**

**won't happen**

a) The south have better weather than the north. (will)
   *The south will have better weather than the north.*
b) Tomorrow probably be warmer than today. (will)
c) I think we have a lot of snow next winter. (will)
d) It rain later today. (might)
e) There be a storm before the weekend. (might)
f) It be sunny tomorrow. (won't)

**2** Rewrite the sentences so that they are true for where you live. Compare with a partner.

**Anecdote**

**1** 🔲 98 You are going to listen to a woman talking about her favorite time of year. Listen and <u>underline</u> the answers she gives.

☐ Which months of the year do you like best?
☐ What season is that in your country?
☐ What is the weather like at that time of year?
☐ What's the countryside like at that time of year?
☐ What do you usually wear at that time of year?
☐ What do you usually do at that time of year?
☐ What do you particularly like about that time of year?

a) I like… (August, December, October, etc.)
b) It's… (spring, summer, fall, winter)
c) It's… (warm but not hot, very sunny, cold, etc.)
d) The countryside is… (green, colorful, snowy, etc.)
e) I usually wear… (light clothes, dressy clothes, etc.)
f) I go… (skiing, to the beach, for walks in the hills, etc.)
g) I like it because… (I'm on vacation /it's beautiful, etc.)

**2** Think about your favorite time of year. You are going to tell your partner about it. Read the questions and sentence beginnings in 1 again and think about what to say and how to say it.

**3** Tell your partner about your favorite time of year.

# Review 4

## Experiences

**Language reviewed:** present perfect (Unit 16); computers (Unit 16); driving (Unit 17); past participles (Unit 16); past continuous (Unit 18); question forms (Unit 17)

**Present perfect**

Hey, Joe, have you seen the mouse?

Sorry I'm so late— I've been stuck in an elevator.

Work with a partner. You are going to find out about your partner's experience with computers and with driving.

- Complete each question with the past participle of the verb in parentheses.
- Complete the *Me* column with *Yes* or *No* and guess the answers for your partner.
- Ask the questions and find out if you were right about your partner's experience.

| Questions | Me | Partner |
|---|---|---|
| **Computer experience** | | |
| a) Have you ever (buy) anything on the Internet? *bought* | | |
| b) Have you ever (download) music from the Internet? | | |
| c) Have you ever (go) to an online auction? | | |
| d) Have you ever (delete) an important file by mistake? | | |
| e) Have you ever (set up) a Web site? | | |
| f) Have you ever (take part) in a chat-room discussion? | | |
| **Driving experience** | | |
| g) Have you ever (be) late because of a traffic jam? | | |
| h) Have you ever (drive) in a foreign country? | | |
| i) Have you ever (get) a parking ticket? | | |
| j) Have you ever (drive) at over 100 mph? | | |
| k) Have you ever (lend) your car to a friend? | | |
| l) Have you ever (lose) your car keys? | | |

**Word stress**

**1** Work with a partner. Say these words from Units 16–19 and underline the stressed syllable. In each group, circle the word with a different stress pattern or different number of syllables from the other two.

a) scenery  volcano  dangerous     d) desert  delete  concert
b) pronounced  surface  happened     e) badly  neatly  regularly
c) pollution  evening  business     f) conversation  expression  preposition

**2** 〔▪▪〕 99 Listen, check, and repeat the answers to 1.

**Past participles**

〔▪▪〕 100 You are going to play bingo. Follow the instructions.

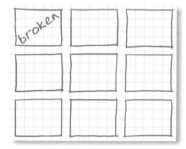

broken

- Copy the bingo card and complete it with the past participle forms of nine different verbs in the box.
- Listen to the recording, and when you hear a verb on your card, ~~cross it out~~.
- When three verbs in a vertical (↓), horizontal (→), or diagonal (↘) line are crossed out, shout, "Bingo!"
- Check your answers with the tapescript on page 127.

| | | | | | | | | | | |
|---|---|---|---|---|---|---|---|---|---|---|
| break | bring | build | catch | do | drive | eat | fall | feel | find | have | hear |
| keep | lend | make | mean | meet | pay | read | sell | shoot | sit | sleep | |
| speak | spend | teach | think | wake | wear | write | | | | | |

**Simple past and past continuous**

**1** Work with a partner. Complete the story with the verb forms in the box. Pred[ict the] ending of the story.

> didn't come    continued    ~~was shooting~~    found    gave    was planning
> shook    was talking    went    went

A Hollywood director (1) *was shooting* an important movie in the desert when an old Native American man (2) ____ up to him and said, "Tomorrow rain."
The next day it rained.

A few days later, the director (3) ____ to the cameraman about the next day's shooting. The Native American went up to him and said, "Tomorrow storm."

He was right again, and he saved the director thousands of dollars.

The director was very impressed and (4) ____ the old man a job.

The old man (5) ____ to predict the weather correctly, but then he (6) ____ for three weeks.

The director (7) ____ to shoot an important scene, and he needed good weather. So he (8) ____ to look for the Native American.

When he (9) ____ the old man, he said, "Listen, I have to shoot an important scene tomorrow. What will the weather be like?"

The old man (10) ____ his head and said, '………'

**2** 🔊 101 Listen and check your answers and ideas in 1.

**Anecdote**

**1** Complete the Anecdote questions with *How, What, When, Where,* and *Who.*

☐ 1 ____ did your trip start and finish?  It was from my house to… (school, my grandparents', etc.)
☐ 2 ____ far was it?  It was… (2 miles, 50 miles, 230 miles, etc.)
☐ 3 ____ did you travel?  I… (walked, biked, went by car, went by bus, etc.)
☐ 4 ____ time did you usually start out?  I usually started out… (at eight o'clock, after school, very early, etc.)
☐ 5 ____ long did it take you?  It took me… (half an hour, six hours, all day, etc.)
☐ 6 ____ kind of terrain did you go through?  I went… (through woods, along the coast, down a hill, etc.)
☐ 7 ____ kinds of buildings did you go past?  I went past… (a church, a supermarket, a monument, etc.)
☐ 8 ____ did you usually travel with?  I traveled… (with my family, with my friends, alone, etc.)
☐ 9 ____ did you usually do on your trip?  I… (looked out the window, slept, listened to music, etc.)
☐ 10 ____ was the last time you took this trip?  It was… (in 1995, three months ago, etc.)

**2** 🔊 102 Think about a trip that you often took when you were younger. You are going to tell a partner about it. Read and listen to the questions and think about your answers.

**3** Think about what to say and how to say it. Use the sentence beginnings to help you.

**4** Tell your partner about your trip.

# The Review Game

**Language reviewed:**
All the main structures
in Units 11–19.

**7**
Talk about
an old friend
from school.

**8**
How far is your
job from your
house?
(page 71)

**9**
How long it does
take you to get
to work?
(page 71)

**10**
All the furniture
made of ice.
(page 80)

**6**
I've been to
New York three
years ago.
(page 69)

FINISH

**5**
I have too
many work.
(page 61)

**4**
You should
be careful.
(page 61)

**3**
Talk about your
house.

**2**
My sister hopes
go to college in
England.
(page 53)

**1**
Is it
raining?
(page 49)

**Player 1**
START

**3**
Talk about your
last summer
vacation.

**2**
I'm going
have a big party.
(page 53)

**1**
We aren't going
to stay for a
long time.
(page 53)

**Player 4**
START

**4**
I'm too
much tired.
(page 61)

**5**
You shouldn't
work so late.
(page 61)

**6**
I've never be
to New York.
(page 69)

FINISH

**7**
Talk about your
favorite time
of year.

**8**
What color are
your eyes?
(page 71)

**9**
What time you
do get up?
(page 71)

**10**
My house was
build before
1980.
(page 80)

**10**
My shoes were designed in Italy. (page 80)

**9**
The beds covered in reindeer skins. (page 80)

**8**
I am sleeping when you called me. (page 77)

**7**
Talk about the last time you went shopping.

**FINISH**

**6**
He's met the love of his life in 1996. (page 69)

**5**
Do you have enough room? (page 61)

**4**
There are too much problems. (page 61)

**Player 2 START**

**1**
Are the birds singing? (page 49)

**2**
We want visit India next year. (page 53)

**3**
Talk about one of your relatives.

**Player 3 START**

**1**
Is he reading? (page 49)

**2**
I'd like climb Mount Fuji in Japan. (page 53)

**3**
Talk about someone you think has a good job.

**4**
I'm not as tall my father. (page 57)

**5**
I don't have money enough. (page 61)

**6**
It's not big enough. (page 61)

**FINISH**

**10**
My salary is pays by check. (page 80)

**9**
How many people can you fit in your car? (page 71)

**8**
You should to get out more. (page 61)

**7**
Talk about the last time you had a delicious meal.

## HOW TO PLAY

Play the game with three, four, or five players. One person in each game is the *Checker*. The *Checker* doesn't play the game. You will need a coin and counters and an extra copy of *American Inside Out* Elementary Student's Book.

1  Each player places his/her counter on a different square marked START.

2  Decide who is going to start the game. The first player tosses the coin and moves the counter along the "road" as follows:
"Heads" = two spaces.
"Tails" = one space.

3  Players then take turns. If a player lands on a grammar square (darker color), he/she must decide if the sentence on that square is grammatically correct or incorrect. If he/she thinks the sentence is incorrect, he/she must correct it.

4  The *Checker* then turns to the Language Reference on the page given to see if the player is right. If the player is right, he/she takes another turn. If the player is wrong, he/she misses a turn.

5  If a player lands on a speaking square (lighter color), he/she must talk about the topic for sixty seconds. The *Checker* times the player from the moment he/she starts speaking.

6  The first player to reach FINISH is the winner.

# Pairwork: Student A

## 11 Looks

**Page 46.
Vocabulary:
description, 4**

You are going to label
the people in picture B.
Their names are *Jason,
Jane, Emma, Max,* and
*Mickey.* Your partner is
going to label the
people in picture A.
Take turns asking
questions.

For example:
*A: Which one is Jason?*
*B: He's black. He has
short dark hair with
blond highlights.*

Marco    Karen                    Lily              Paul    Susanna

1 _____    2 _____    3 _____    4 _____    5 _____

## 11 Looks

### Page 49. Close-up. Present continuous, 3

You are going to mime three of the following activities. Your partner is going to mime different activities.
Take turns guessing what your partner is miming.

a)  You are eating an ice-cream.
b)  You are watching a horror movie.
c)  You are doing the ironing.
d)  You are putting on ski boots.
e)  You are waiting to see the dentist.
f)  You are having a cold shower.

## 12 Reality

### Page 52. Close-up. *(be) going to*, 5

You and your partner are going to compare your plans for the immediate future.

* Answer the questions and complete the *Me* column with a ✔, ✗, or ? according to the key.
* Ask your partner the same questions and complete the *My partner* column.
* Discuss your answers. Are you more sure or less sure about your plans than your partner?

| Questions | Me | My partner | Key |
|---|---|---|---|
| a)  Are you going to walk home after class? | _____ | _____ | ✔ = Yes, I am. |
| b)  Are you going to send any e-mails this evening? | _____ | _____ | ✗ = No, I'm not. |
| c)  Are you going to have lunch at home tomorrow? | _____ | _____ | ? = I'm not sure. |
| d)  Are you going to go out on Saturday night? | _____ | _____ | |
| e)  Are you going to do any studying in the next few days? | _____ | _____ | |
| f)  Are you going to go anywhere interesting next week? | _____ | _____ | |

# 13 Things

## Page 56. Close-up. Superlatives, 2

You are going to take a quiz about your town/city.

- Complete each question with the correct superlative form and add a question of your own.
- Answer the questions with your own ideas in the *Me* column.
- Ask your partner the questions and write your partner's answers in the *My partner* column.
- Discuss your ideas.

### Town/City Quiz

| Questions | Me | My partner |
|---|---|---|
| a) Which is the (ugly) *ugliest* building? | _____ | _____ |
| b) Which is the (famous) park? | _____ | _____ |
| c) Which is the (old) monument? | _____ | _____ |
| d) Which is the (expensive) street? | _____ | _____ |
| e) Which is the (big) supermarket? | _____ | _____ |
| f) Which is the (popular) restaurant? | _____ | _____ |
| g) Which is the ___ ? | _____ | _____ |

# 14 Energy

## Page 59. Vocabulary: frequency expressions, 3

You are going to compare good and bad habits with your partner. You are going to ask your partner about good habits. Your partner is going to ask you about bad habits.

- Complete the *Me* column with frequency expressions to make the sentences true for you.
- Ask your partner questions beginning: *How often ...?* and complete the *My partner* column.
  For example: *A: How often do you exercise?   B: Twice a week.*
- Discuss your answers. Are you and your partner the same (✓) or different (✗)?

### Good Habits

| Me | My partner | ✓ = We're the same. ✗ = We're different. |
|---|---|---|
| a) I do some exercise ___ . | _____ | _____ |
| b) I eat fruit ___ . | _____ | _____ |
| c) I drink water ___ . | _____ | _____ |
| d) I take a vacation ___ . | _____ | _____ |
| e) I go to the dentist ___ . | _____ | _____ |
| f) I listen to relaxing music ___ . | _____ | _____ |

# 16 dotcom

## Page 67. Reading

You are going to find out about how two old friends got back in touch with each other.

- Read the two e-mails and fill in the blanks, using the words in the box. Check your answers with Student B.

> band    cassette    Darren    garage    Pamela    party    phone    Purple

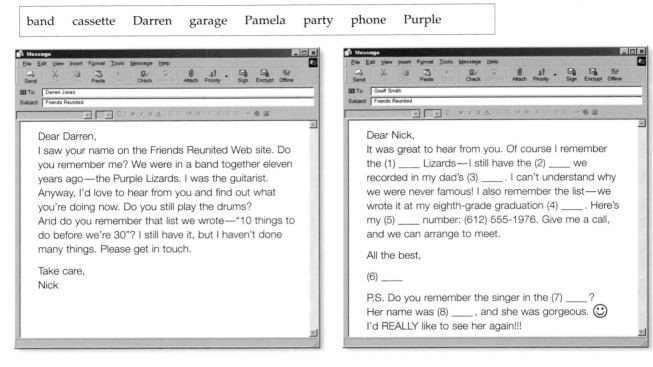

- You and your partner have alternate lines of a summary of the e-mail exchange. Complete the summary with your own ideas first and then check with your partner.

| | | |
|---|---|---|
| a) Nick saw Darren's | e) guitarist, and Darren played | h) ____ |
| b) *name on the Friends Reunited* | f) ____ | i) Nick to give him a |
| c) Web site. They played in a | g) list—"10 things to | j) ____ . |
| d) ____ | | |

- When was the last time you got in touch with an old friend? Tell your partner.

# 16 dotcom

## Page 69. Close-up. Present perfect, 4

You are going to talk to your partner about things you've both done.

- Complete the *Me* column to make the sentences true for you. Add one sentence of your own.
- Ask your partner questions beginning: *What's the…?* and complete the *My partner* column.
  For example: *A: What's the best Web site you've ever visited?  B: Uh, probably the World News one. It's amazing.*
- Discuss your answers.

| Me | My partner |
|---|---|
| a) The best Web site I've ever visited is ___ . | The best Web site he/she's visited is _____ . |
| b) The best book I've ever read is ___ . | _____ |
| c) The best party I've ever been to is ___ . | _____ |
| d) The best-looking woman I've ever seen is ___ . | _____ |
| e) The best meal I've ever had is ___ . | _____ |
| f) The most dangerous sport I've ever tried is ___ . | _____ |
| g) ___ . | _____ |

# 17 Drive

## Page 71. Close-up. Questions with *How* + adverb/adjective and *What* + noun, 3

You are going to ask questions and compare information about you and your partner.

- Read the *Who* questions in column A, and complete the *How* and *What* questions in column B, which will give you the information you want about you and your partner.
- Ask your partner the questions in column B and circle the appropriate answer (*Me* or *My partner*) in column A.
- Compare your answers with other students. Find out the answer to each question in column A for the class.

| A: Who...?—Me or my partner? | B |
|---|---|
| a) Who travels by train the most? (*Me / My partner*) | How often *do you travel by train?* |
| b) Who gets up the earliest in the morning? (*Me / My partner*) | What time ____ ? |
| c) Who has the fastest car? (*Me / My partner*) | How fast ____ ? |
| d) Who spends the most money on traveling every week? (*Me / My partner*) | How much ____ ? |
| e) Who lives the farthest from school? (*Me / My partner*) | How far ____ ? |
| f) Who takes the longest to get to work/school? (*Me / My partner*) | How long ____ ? |

# 18 Justice

## Page 76. Punctuation, 2

You have some lines of the story, *Usher's Revenge,* and Student B has the other lines.

- Take turns dictating your lines to each other, including punctuation and capital letters.
- Complete and then compare your stories. They should be identical.
- What was the usher's revenge?

*Usher's Revenge*
**A:** A man arrived at the theater
**B:** ____
**A:** but his seat was too far
**B:** ____
**A:** So he said to the usher,
**B:** ____
**A:** and I'll give you a generous tip."
**B:** ____
**A:** and the man gave him 25 cents.
**B:** ____
**A:** and then he bent down and whispered to the man,
**B:** ____

# Additional material

## 11 Looks

**Page 48. Reading, 3**

1 b   2 a   3 c   4 a   5 c   6 b   7 b   8 b   9 c   10 b   11 a   12 c

## 12 Reality

**Page 52. Close-up. *want to, 'd (would) like to, hope to*, 3**

Work in groups of three. Choose five pictures (or draw your own in box *l*) and tell your partners how they represent your dreams.

## 13 Things

**Page 54. Reading, 2**

| The top ten things (in order) | | | | |
|---|---|---|---|---|
| 1 money | 3 a TV remote | 5 a wedding ring | 7 glasses | 9 a cellphone |
| 2 keys | 4 gloves | 6 a handbag | 8 an address book | 10 a pet |

# 13 Things

## Page 54. Listening, 3

Work with a partner and follow the instructions.

- Match the descriptions (*a–l*) to the bags (*1–9*). Each description may refer to more than one bag.
- Take turns to choose a bag.
- Ask questions like the questions in Listening 2 on page 54 to find out which bag your partner chose.

a) It's brown-and-white check.  *4*
b) It's a shopping bag.
c) It has a long strap.
d) It's huge.
e) It's a laptop bag.
f) It's made of plastic.
g) It has some clothes in it.
h) It has the letters CD on the handle.
i) It's made of leather.
j) It's not very big.
k) It's black with a white stripe.
l) It has two pockets on the front.

# Pairwork: Student B

## 11 Looks

**Page 46. Vocabulary: description, 4**

You are going to label the people in picture A. Their names are *Karen, Marco, Paul, Lily,* and *Susanna.* Your partner is going to label the people in picture B. Take turns asking questions.

For example:
*A: Which one is Karen?*
*B: She has short straight hair. She has big earrings.*

1 ____  2 ____        3 ____        4 ____  5 ____

Jane        Emma        Mickey        Jason        Max

## 11 Looks

**Page 49. Close-up. Present continuous, 3**

You are going to mime three of the following activities. Your partner is going to mime different activities. Take turns guessing what your partner is miming.

a) You are eating spaghetti.
b) You are watching a funny movie.
c) You are doing the dishes.
d) You are putting on lipstick.
e) You are waiting for a bus.
f) You are swimming in a pool.

## 12 Reality

**Page 52. Close-up. *(be) going to*, 5**

You and your partner are going to compare your plans for the immediate future.

* Answer the questions and complete the *Me* column with a ✓, ✗, or ? according to the key.
* Ask your partner the same questions and complete the *My partner* column.
* Discuss your answers. Are you more sure or less sure about your plans than your partner?

| Questions | Me | My partner | Key |
|---|---|---|---|
| a) Are you going to drive home after class? | ____ | ____ | ✓ = Yes, I am. |
| b) Are you going to cook dinner tonight? | ____ | ____ | ✗ = No, I'm not. |
| c) Are you going to have lunch in a restaurant tomorrow? | ____ | ____ | ? = I'm not sure. |
| d) Are you going to go out on Friday night? | ____ | ____ | |
| e) Are you going to get some exercise in the next few days? | ____ | ____ | |
| f) Are you going to do anything interesting next week? | ____ | ____ | |

# 13 Things

## Page 56. Close-up. Superlatives, 2

You are going to take a quiz about your town/city.

- Complete each question with the correct superlative form and add a question of your own.
- Answer the questions with your own ideas in the *Me* column.
- Ask your partner the questions and write your partner's answers in the *My partner* column.
- Discuss your ideas.

### Town/City Quiz

| Questions | Me | My partner |
|---|---|---|
| a) Which is the (interesting) *most interesting* building? | ___ | ___ |
| b) Which is the (beautiful) park? | ___ | ___ |
| c) Which is the (modern) monument? | ___ | ___ |
| d) Which is the (busy) street? | ___ | ___ |
| e) Which is the (cheap) supermarket? | ___ | ___ |
| f) Which is the (quiet) restaurant? | ___ | ___ |
| g) Which is the ___? | ___ | ___ |

# 14 Energy

## Page 59. Vocabulary: frequency expressions, 3

You are going to compare good and bad habits with your partner. You are going to ask your partner about bad habits. Your partner is going to ask you about good habits.

- Complete the *Me* column with frequency expressions to make the sentences true for you.
- Ask your partner questions beginning: *How often...?* and complete the *My partner* column.
  For example: *A: How often do you get to work/school late?   B: Once a month.*
- Discuss your answers. Are you and your partner the same (✓) or different (✗)?

### Bad Habits

| Me | My partner | ✓ = We're the same.<br>✗ = We're different. |
|---|---|---|
| a) I get to work/school late ___. | ___ | ___ |
| b) I eat fast food ___. | ___ | ___ |
| c) I work late at night ___. | ___ | ___ |
| d) I drink alcohol ___. | ___ | ___ |
| e) I stay up all night ___. | ___ | ___ |
| f) I get up late ___. | ___ | ___ |

# 16 dotcom

## Page 67. Reading

You are going to find out about how two old friends got back in touch with each other.

- Read the two e-mails and fill in the blanks, using the words in the box. Check your answers with Student A.

> 30    drums    eleven    Friends    Nick    guitarist    list    Lizards

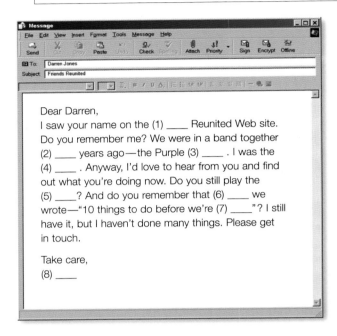

Dear Darren,
I saw your name on the (1) _____ Reunited Web site.
Do you remember me? We were in a band together
(2) _____ years ago—the Purple (3) _____ . I was the
(4) _____ . Anyway, I'd love to hear from you and find
out what you're doing now. Do you still play the
(5) _____? And do you remember that (6) _____ we
wrote—"10 things to do before we're (7) _____"? I still
have it, but I haven't done many things. Please get
in touch.

Take care,
(8) _____

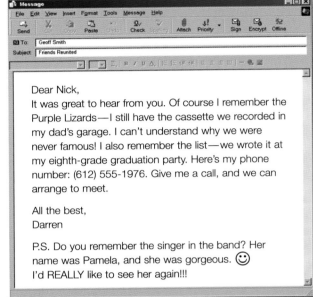

Dear Nick,
It was great to hear from you. Of course I remember the
Purple Lizards—I still have the cassette we recorded in
my dad's garage. I can't understand why we were
never famous! I also remember the list—we wrote it at
my eighth-grade graduation party. Here's my phone
number: (612) 555-1976. Give me a call, and we can
arrange to meet.

All the best,
Darren

P.S. Do you remember the singer in the band? Her
name was Pamela, and she was gorgeous. ☺
I'd REALLY like to see her again!!!

- You and your partner have alternate lines of a summary of the email exchange. Complete the summary with your own ideas first and then check with your partner.

  a) *Nick saw Darren's*
  b) name on the Friends Reunited
  c) _____
  d) band in high school. Nick was the

  e) _____
  f) the drums. They wrote a
  g) _____

  h) do before we're 30." Darren asks
  i) _____
  j) call so they can arrange to meet.

- When was the last time you got in touch with an old friend? Tell your partner.

# 16 dotcom

## Page 69. Close-up. Present perfect, 4

You are going to talk to your partner about things you've both done.

- Complete the *Me* column to make the sentences true for you. Add one sentence of your own.
- Ask your partner questions beginning: *What's the…?* and complete the *My partner* column.
  For example: *B: What's the best computer game you've ever played? A: Uh, Tomb Raider. It's fantastic.*
- Discuss your answers.

| Me | My partner |
|---|---|
| a) The best computer game I've ever played is ___. | The best computer game he/she's ever played is _____ . |
| b) The best movie I've ever seen is ___ . | _____ |
| c) The best live concert I've ever been to is ___. | _____ |
| d) The best-looking man I've ever seen is ___. | _____ |
| e) The strangest food I've ever eaten is ___. | _____ |
| f) The most beautiful place I've ever been to is ___. | _____ |
| g) _____ | _____ |

# 17 Drive

## Page 71. Close-up. Questions with *How* + adverb/adjective and *What* + noun, 3

You are going to ask questions and compare information about you and your partner.

- Read the *Who* questions in column A, and complete the *How* and *What* questions in column B, which will give you the information you want about you and your partner.
- Ask your partner the questions in column B and (circle) the appropriate answer (*Me* or *My partner*) in column A.
- Compare your answers with other students. Find out the answer to each question in column A for the class.

| A: Who...?—Me or my partner? | B |
|---|---|
| a) Who travels by bus the most? (*Me/My partner*) | How often *do you travel by bus*? |
| b) Who starts work the earliest? (*Me/My partner*) | What time _____ ? |
| c) Who has the oldest car? (*Me/My partner*) | How old _____ ? |
| d) Who can fit the most people in his/her car? (*Me/My partner*) | How many _____ ? |
| e) Who lives the farthest from downtown? (*Me/My partner*) | How far _____ ? |
| f) Who takes the longest to get ready in the morning? (*Me/My partner*) | How long _____ ? |

# 18 Justice

## Page 76. Punctuation, 2

You have some lines of the story, *Usher's Revenge,* and Student A has the other lines.

- Take turns dictating your lines to each other, including punctuation and capital letters.
- Complete and then compare your stories. They should be identical.
- What was the usher's revenge?

*Usher's Revenge*

**A:** _____
**B:** to see a mystery play,
**A:** _____
**B:** from the stage.
**A:** _____
**B:** "Find me a better seat
**A:** _____
**B:** The usher moved him into the front row
**A:** _____
**B:** The usher looked at his tip for a minute,
**A:** _____
**B:** "The wife did it!"

# Word list

## Unit 11

accessory (-ies) *n C* /ək'sɛsəri/
average *adj* /'ævərɪdʒ/ ★★
**beard** *n C* /'bird/
beautiful *adj* /'byutɪfʊl/ ★★★
blond *adj* /bland/ ★
**bracelet** *n C* /'breislət/
casual *adj* /'kæʒuəl/ ★★
chain *n C* /tʃein/

### Clothes

belt *n C* /bɛlt/ ★★
boot *n C* /but/ ★★★
coat *n C* /kout/ ★★★
dress (-es) *n C* /drɛs/ ★★★
footwear *n N* /'fʊtwær/
hat *n C* /hæt/ ★★★
jacket *n C* /'dʒækət/ ★★★
jeans *npl* /dʒinz/ ★
pants *npl* /pænts/ ★★
shirt *n C* /ʃərt/ ★★★
shoe *n C* /ʃu/ ★★★
sneaker *n C* /'snikər/
sock *n C* /sak/ ★
suit *n C* /sut/ ★★★
sweater *n C* /'swɛtər/ ★★
sweatsuit *n C* /'swɛtsut/
tie *n C* /tai/ ★★★
top *n C* /tap/ ★★★
T-shirt *n C* /'ti ʃərt/ ★
underwear *n N* /'ʌndərwær/ ★

curly *adj* /'kərli/
earring *n C* /'irɪŋ/ ★
eye *n C* /ai/ ★★★
face *n C* /feis/ ★★★
get (out of sth) *v* /gɛt/ ★★★
**get dressed** /gɛt 'drɛst/
glasses *npl* /'glæsəz/ ★
hair *n N* /hær/ ★★★
handsome *adj* /'hæn(d)səm/ ★★
**have a good time** /hæv ə gʊd 'taim/
head *n C* /hɛd/ ★★★
highlights *npl* /'hailaits/
hold (held, held) *v* /hould/ ★★★
lipstick *n C* /'lɪpstɪk/
long *adj* /laŋ/ ★★★
**look like** *v* /'lʊk laik/
lovely *adj* /'lʌvli/
**medium-length** *adj* /'midiəm lɛŋθ/
mustache *n C* /'məstæʃ/ ★★★
pretty *adj* /'prɪti/ ★★
put (sth on) (put, put) *v* /pʊt/ ★★★
quiz (-zes) *n C* /kwɪz/
shaved *adj* /ʃeivd/
short *adj* /ʃɔrt/ ★★★
smile *n C* /smail/ ★★★
spiky *adj* /'spaiki/
straight *adj* /streit/ ★★
sunglasses *npl* /'sʌnglæsɪz/
take (sth off) (took, taken) *v* /teik/ ★★★
tattoo *n C* /tæ'tu/
try (sth on) (tried, tried) *v* /trai/ ★★★
wait (for sb/sth) *v* /weit/ ★★★
wave *v* /weiv/ ★★
wavy *adj* /'weivi/
wear (wore, wore) *v* /wær/ ★★★

## Unit 12

application form *n C* /æplɪ'keiʃ(ə)n fɔrm/
appointment *n C* /ə'pointmənt/ ★★★
believe (in sb/sth) *v* /bɪ'liv/ ★★★
cope (with sb/sth) *v* /koup/ ★★
definitely *adv* /'dɛfənɪtli/ ★★
diamond *adj* /'daiəmənd/ ★★
**fairy tale** *n C* /'færi teil/
film *v* /fɪlm/ ★
future *adj* /'fyutʃər/ ★★★
future *n C* /'fyutʃər/ ★★★
**hobby** (-ies) *n C* /'habi/
**honeymoon** *n C* /'hʌnimun/
hope *v* /houp/ ★★★
list *n C* /lɪst/ ★★★
participate *v* /par'tɪsɪpeit/ ★★

photo album *n C* /'foutou ælbəm/
plan *n C* /plæn/ ★★★
positive *adj* /'pazɪtɪv/ ★★★
program *n C* /'prougræm/ ★★★

### TV programs

documentary (-ies) *n C* /dakyə'mɛntəri/ ★
**game show** *n C* /'geim ʃou/
news *n N* /nuz/ ★★★
**reality TV** *n N* /ri'æləti ti 'vi/
**soap opera** *n C* /'soup ap(ə)rə/
**sports program** *n C* /'sports prougræm/
**talk show** *n C* /'tɔk ʃou/ ★
weather *n N* /'wɛðər/ ★★★

rose *n C* /rouz/ ★★★
stream *n C* /strim/ ★★
successful *adj* /sək'sɛsful/ ★★★
traditional *adj* /trə'dɪʃ(ə)nəl/ ★★★

## Unit 13

**address book** *n C* /ə'drɛs bʊk/
afford *v* /ə'fɔrd/ ★★★
bad *adj* /bæd/ ★★★
big *adj* /bɪg/ ★★★
**bikini** *n C* /bɪ'kini/
bill *n C* /bɪl/ ★★★
busy *adj* /'bɪzi/ ★★★
cash *n N* /kæʃ/ ★★★
check *n C* /tʃɛk/ ★★★
debt *n C* /dɛt/ ★★★
far *adj* /far/ ★★★
fast *adj* /fæst/ ★★★
generous *adj* /'dʒɛn(ə)rəs/ ★★
glove *n C* /glʌv/ ★★
**handbag** *n C* /'hændbæg/
hot *adj* /hat/ ★★★
hundred *num* /'hʌndrəd/ ★★
key *n C* /ki/ ★★★
**laptop computer** *n C* /læptap kəm'pyutər/
**lost-and-found** *n N* /lɔst ən(d) 'faund/
lucky *adj* /'lʌki/ ★★★
million *num* /'mɪlyən/ ★★
neighbor *n C* /'neibər/ ★★
object *n C* /'abdʒɛkt/ ★★★
pay (sth/sb off) *v* /pei/ ★★★
poor *adj* /pɔr/ ★★★
popular *adj* /'papyələr/ ★★★
quiet *adj* /'kwaiət/ ★★★
relaxed *adj* /rɪ'lækst/ ★
save *v* /seiv/ ★★★
**save money** /seiv 'mʌni/

Based on data from the *Macmillan Essential Dictionary*

set (sth up) (set, set) v /sɛt/ ★★★
size n C /saiz/ ★★★
slow adj /slou/ ★★★
snake n C /sneik/
swear (swore, sworn) v /swær/ ★
tall adj /tɔl/ ★★★
thousand num /'θauz(ə)nd/ ★★
TV remote n C /ti vi rɪ'mout/
ugly adj /ʌgli/ ★
violent adj /'vaiələnt/ ★★★
Web site n C /'wɛb sait/ ★★
wedding ring n C /'wɛdɪŋ rɪŋ/
young adj /yʌŋ/ ★★★

# Unit 14

ancestry n C /'ænsɛstri/
bend (bent, bent) v /bɛnd/ ★★
body (-ies) n C /'badi/ ★★★

## Parts of the body

arm n C /ɑrm/ ★★★
back n C /bæk/ ★★★
chest n C /tʃɛst/ ★★★
chin n C /tʃɪn/ ★★
ear n C /ir/ ★★★
finger n C /'fɪŋgər/ ★★★
foot (feet) n C /fʊt/ ★★★
hand n C /hænd/ ★★★
heart n C /hɑrt/ ★★★
hip n C /hɪp/ ★★
knee n C /ni/ ★★★
leg n C /lɛg/ ★★★
lip n C /lɪp/ ★★★
neck n C /nɛk/ ★★★
nose n C /nouz/ ★★★
shoulder n C /'ʃouldər/ ★★★
stomach n C /'stʌmək/ ★★
thumb n C /θʌm/ ★★
toe n C /tou/ ★★
tooth (teeth) n C /tuθ/ ★★★
waist n C /weist/ ★★

charming adj /'tʃɑrmɪŋ/
clap (clapped, clapped) v /klæp/
click v /klɪk/
cold n C /kould/ ★★
cross v /krɔs/ ★★★
crowded adj /'kraudɪd/ ★
energy n N /'ɛnərdʒi/ ★★★
exciting adj /ɪk'saitɪŋ/ ★★
flamenco n N /flə'mɛŋkou/
fold v /fould/ ★★★
go dancing /gou 'dænsɪŋ/
gypsy (-ies) n C /'dʒɪpsi/
hairdresser n C /'hærdrɛsər/ ★
headache n C /'hɛdeik/ ★
impulsive adj /ɪm'pʌlsɪv/

loyal adj /'lɔiəl/ ★★
nod (nodded, nodded) v /nad/ ★★★
once adv /wʌns/ ★★★
perform v /pər'fɔrm/ ★★★
performance n C /pər'fɔrməns/ ★★★
pushy n C /'pʊʃi/
questionnaire n C /kwɛstʃyə'nær/
score n C /skɔr/ ★★★
selfish adj /'sɛlfɪʃ/
shrug (shrugged, shrugged) v /ʃrʌg/
soul n C /soul/ ★★★
stamp v /stæmp/ ★★
stomachache n C /'stʌməkeik/
touch v /tʌtʃ/ ★★★
twice adv /twais/ ★★★
unsociable adj /ʌn'souʃəb(ə)l/

# Unit 15

fitting room n C /'fɪtɪŋ rum/
go sightseeing /gou 'saitsiɪŋ/
noisy adj /'nɔisi/ ★
runner n C /'rʌnər/ ★★
safe adj /seif/ ★★★
suit v /sut/ ★★★
take a day off /teik ə dei 'ɔf/

# Unit 16

band n C /bænd/ ★★★
classmate n C /'klæsmeit/
delete v /dɪ'lit/
desktop n C /'dɛsktap/ ★★
download v /'daunloud/
drums npl /drʌmz/
elementary school n C /ɛlə'mɛntəri skul/ ★
employ v /ɪm'plɔi/ ★★★
file n C /fail/ ★★★
find (out) (found, found) v /faind/ ★★★
garage n C /gə'raʒ/ ★★
get in touch (with sb/sth) v /gɛt ɪn 'tʌtʃ/
give (sth up) (gave, given) v /gɪv/ ★★★
go online v /gou an'lain/
guitarist n C /gɪ'tarɪst/
humor n N /'hyumər/ ★★
icon n C /'aikan/ ★
Internet n C /'ɪntərnɛt/ ★★★
log on v /lag 'an/
look (after sb/sth) v /lʊk/ ★★★
mouse (mice) n C /maus/ ★★
order v /'ɔrdər/ ★★★
personal organizer n C /pərsən(ə)l 'ɔrgənaizər/
pregnant adj /'prɛgnənt/ ★★
publicity n N /pʌb'lɪs(ə)ti/ ★★
record v /rɪ'kɔrd/ ★★★
reunion n C /ri'yunyən/
reunite v /riyu'nait/
screen n C /skrin/ ★★★
search (for sb/th) v /sərtʃ/ ★★★

sell (sold, sold) v /sɛl/ ★★★
send (sent, sent) v /sɛnd/ ★★★
send an e-mail /sɛnd ən 'imeil/
sense n C /sɛns/ ★★★
sense of humor n C /sɛns əv 'hyumər/
surf v /sərf/ ★
surf the Net /sərf ðə 'nɛt/
take (sth on) (took, taken) v /teik/ ★★★
ticket n C /'tɪkɪt/ ★★★
toolbar n C /'tulbar/
word of mouth n N /wərd əv 'mauθ/

# Unit 17

coast n /koust/ ★★
construction n N /kən'strʌkʃən/ ★★★
double-park v /'dʌb(ə)l park/
drive n C /draiv/ ★★★
drive (drove, driven) v /draiv/ ★★★
drive (sb) crazy /draiv sʌmbədi 'kreizi/
get stuck /gɛt 'stʌk/
go (went, gone) v /gou/ ★★★

## go + prepositions of movement

go across /gou ə'krɔs/
go along /gou ə'lɔŋ/
go down /gou 'daun/
go into /gou 'ɪntu/
go out of /gou 'aut əv/
go over /gou 'ouvər/
go past /gou 'pæst/
go straight /gou 'streit/
go through /gou 'θru/
go up /gou 'ʌp/

have an accident /hæv ən 'æksɪdənt/
highway n C /'haiwei/ ★★
journey n C /'dʒərni/ ★★★
lighthouse n C /'laithaus/

## Ordinal numbers

first num /fərst/ ★★★
second num /'sɛk(ə)nd/ ★★★
third num /θərd/
fourth num /fɔrθ/
fifth num /fɪfθ/
sixth num /sɪksθ/
seventh num /'sɛv(ə)nθ/
eighth num /eitθ/
ninth num /nainθ/
tenth num /tɛnθ/

pass v /pæs/ ★★★
plane n C /plein/ ★★★
rush hour n C /'rʌʃ auər/
scenery n N /'sinəri/ ★
start (out) v /start/ ★★★

stand (stood, stood) v /stænd/ ★★★
– I can't stand it when …
  /aɪ kænt 'stænd ɪt wɛn …/
traffic lights npl /'træfɪk laɪts/
travel abroad v /træv(ə)l ə'brɔd/
turn left/right v /tərn 'lɛft, raɪt/

## Unit 18

angrily adv /'æŋgrɪli/
attractive adj /ə'træktɪv/ ★★★
attractively adv /ə'træktɪvli/
badly adv /'bædli/ ★★★
beautifully adv /'byutɪf(ə)li/
careful adj /'kærf(ə)l/ ★★★
carefully adv /'kærf(ə)li/
castle n C /'kæs(ə)l/ ★
catch (caught, caught) v /kætʃ/ ★★★
differently adv /'dɪfrəntli/
dinner party (-ies) n C /'dɪnər parti/
evil adj /'iv(ə)l/ ★★
finally adv /'faɪnəli/ ★★★
frog n C /frag/ ★
have an affair /hæv ən ə'fær/
justice n N /'dʒʌstɪs/ ★★★
kiss (-es) n C /kɪs/ ★★
loudly adv /'laudli/
mystery play n C /'mɪstəri pleɪ/
neatly adj /'nitli/
next adv /nɛkst/ ★★★
once upon a time /'wʌns əpɑn ə 'taɪm/
paint n N /peɪnt/ ★★
plastic adj /'plæstɪk/ ★★★
pond n C /pɑnd/
pot n C /pɑt/ ★★
prince n C /prɪns/ ★★
princess (-es) n C /'prɪnsɛs/ ★★
quick adj /kwɪk/ ★★★
quickly adv /'kwɪkli/ ★★★
quietly adv /'kwaɪətli/ ★★★
revenge n N /rɪ'vɛndʒ/
row n C /rou/ ★★★
salt n N /sɔlt/ ★ ★
scissors npl /'sɪzərz/ ★
shoplifter n C /'ʃɑplɪftər/
stage n C /steɪdʒ/ ★★★
steal (stole, stolen) v /stil/ ★★
then adv /ðɛn/ ★★★
tip n C /tɪp/ ★★
unhappily adv /ʌn'hæpɪli/
unhappy adj /ʌn'hæpi/ ★★
usher n C /'ʌʃər/
watch (-es) n C /watʃ/ ★★
well adv /wɛl/ ★★★
whisper v /'wɪspər/ ★★
wine n N /waɪn/ ★★★
witch (-es) n C /wɪtʃ/ ★

## Unit 19

cliff n C /klɪf/ ★★
construct v /kən'strʌkt/ ★★★
countryside n C /'kʌntrisaɪd/ ★
desert n C /'dɛzərt/ ★★
design v /dɪ'zaɪn/ ★★★
extremely adv /ɪk'strimli/ ★★★
Fahrenheit n N /'færənheit/
field n C /fild/ ★★★
geography n N /dʒi'agrəfi/
glacier n C /'gleiʃər/
ice n N /aɪs/ ★★★
invite v /ɪn'vaɪt/ ★★★
melt v /mɛlt/ ★★
month n C /mʌnθ/ ★★★
planet n C /'plænɪt/ ★★
poem n C /'pouəm/ ★★
rainbow n C /'reinbou/
reindeer n C /'reindɪr/
season n C /'siz(ə)n/ ★★★

---
**Seasons**

spring n C /sprɪŋ/ ★★★
summer n C /'sʌmər/ ★★★
fall n C /'fɔl/ ★★★
winter n C /'wɪntər/ ★★★

---

shore n C /ʃɔr/ ★★
situate v /'sɪtʃueɪt/
sleeping bag n C /'slipɪŋ bæg/
space n N /speɪs/ ★★★
sun n N /sʌn/ ★★★
temperature n N /'tɛmp(ə)rətʃʊr/ ★★★
visitor n C /'vɪzɪtər/ ★★★
volcano (-es) n C /vɑl'keinou/ ★

---
**Weather**

cloud n C /klaud/ ★★★
cloudy adj /'klaudi/
cool adj /kul/ ★★★
fog n N /fag/ ★
foggy adj /'fagi/
freezing adj /'frizɪŋ/
nice adj /naɪs/ ★★★
overcast adj /'ouvərkæst/
rain n N /rein/ ★★★
rain v /rein/ ★★
rainy adj /'reini/
snow n N /snou/ ★★★
storm n C /stɔrm/ ★★
stormy adj /'stɔrmi/
wind n N /wɪnd/ ★★★
windy adj /'wɪndi/

---

weather forecast n C /'wɛðər fɔrkæst/

## Unit 20

bike v /baɪk/
by car/bus adv
  /baɪ kar, bʌs/
continue v /kən'tɪnyu/ ★★★
director n C /dɪ'rɛktər/ ★★★
lend (lent, lent) v /lɛnd/ ★★
monument n C /'manyəmənt/
Native American n C /neɪtɪv ə'mɛrɪk(ə)n/
parking ticket n C /'parkɪŋ tɪkɪt/
plan (planned, planned) v /plæn/ ★★★
scene n C /sin/ ★★★
shake (shook, shaken) v /ʃeik/ ★★★
woods npl /wʊdz/

Based on data from the *Macmillan Essential Dictionary*

# Verb structures

## Present continuous
**See Unit 11.**

| Affirmative | Negative | Question | Short answer *Yes* | Short answer *No* |
|---|---|---|---|---|
| I'm (am) talking. | I'm not (am not) talking. | Am I talking? | Yes, I am. | No, I'm not. |
| You/We/They're (are) talking. | You/We/They're not (are not) talking. | Are you/we/they talking? | Yes, you/we/they are. | No, you/we/they aren't. |
| He/She/It's (is) talking. | He/She/It isn't (is not) talking. | Is he/she/it talking? | Yes, he/she/it is. | No, he/she/it isn't. |

Note: When a verb ends with a single vowel letter followed by a single consonant letter, you usually double the final consonant letter before -ing: *chat – chatting; jog – jogging; refer – referring; stop – stopping*. An exception in American English is with some verbs of more than one syllable when the stress is not on the syllable immediately before -ing: *cancel – canceling; travel – traveling*.

## Present perfect
**See Unit 16.**

| Affirmative | Negative | Question | Short answer *Yes* | Short answer *No* |
|---|---|---|---|---|
| I/You/We/They've (have) talked. | I/You/We/They haven't (have not) talked. | Have I/you/we/they talked? | Yes, I/you/we/they have. | No, I/you/we/they haven't. |
| He/She/It's (has) talked. | He/She/It hasn't (has not) talked. | Has he/she/it talked? | Yes, he/she/it has. | No, he/she/it hasn't. |

Note: See list of irregular verbs on page B102.

## Past continuous
**See Unit 18.**

| Affirmative | Negative | Question | Short answer *Yes* | Short answer *No* |
|---|---|---|---|---|
| I/He/She/It was talking. | I/He/She/It wasn't (was not) talking. | Was I/he/she/it talking? | Yes, I/he/she/it was. | No, I/he/she/it wasn't. |
| You/We/They were talking. | You/We/They weren't (were not) talking. | Were you/we/they talking? | Yes, you/we/they were. | No, you/we/they weren't. |

## Future: *(be) going to*
**See Unit 12.**

| Affirmative | Negative | Question | Short answer *Yes* | Short answer *No* |
|---|---|---|---|---|
| I'm (am) going to talk. | I'm not (am not) going to talk. | Am I going to talk? | Yes, I am. | No, I'm not. |
| You/We/They're (are) going to talk. | You/We/They're not (are not) going to talk. | Are you/we/they going to talk? | Yes, you/we/they are. | No, you/we/they aren't. |
| He/She/It's (is) going to talk. | He/She/It isn't (is not) going to talk. | Is he/she/it going to talk? | Yes, he/she/it is. | No, he/she/it isn't. |

## Modals

| Affirmative | Negative | Question | Short answer *Yes* | Short answer *No* |
|---|---|---|---|---|
| *might*: see Unit 19. I/You/He, *etc.* **might talk**. | I/You/He, *etc.* **mightn't (might not) talk**. | **Might** I/you/he, *etc.* **talk?** | Yes, I/you/he, *etc.* **might**. | No, I/you/he, *etc.* **might not**. |
| *should*: see Unit 14. I/You/He, *etc.* **should talk**. | I/You/He, *etc.* **shouldn't (should not) talk**. | **Should** I/you/he, *etc.* **talk?** | Yes, I/you/he, *etc.* **should**. | No, I/you/he, *etc.* **shouldn't**. |
| *will*: see Unit 19. I/You/He, *etc.* **'ll (will) talk**. | I/You/He, *etc.* **won't (will not) talk**. | **Will** I/you/he, *etc.* **talk?** | Yes, I/you/he, *etc.* **will**. | No, I/you/he, *etc.* **won't**. |

## Active and passive forms
**See Unit 19.**

| | Active form | Passive form |
|---|---|---|
| **Present** | Somebody **produces** cars. | Cars **are produced**. |
| **Past** | Somebody **produced** cars. | Cars **were produced**. |

# *Adjectives*

## Comparatives
**See Unit 13.**

| + *-er* / *-r* | double letter + *-er* | – *y* + *-ier* | irregular | *more* + **adjective** |
|---|---|---|---|---|
| rich → rich**er** nice → nic**er** | big → big**ger** | lucky → luck**ier** | good → **better** bad → **worse** far → **farther** | generous → **more** generous |

## Superlatives
**See Unit 13.**

| + *-est* / *-st* | double letter + *-est* | – *y* + *-iest* | irregular | *more* + **adjective** |
|---|---|---|---|---|
| rich → the rich**est** nice → the nic**est** | big → the big**gest** | lucky → the luck**iest** | good → the **best** bad → the **worst** far → the **farthest** | generous → the **most** generous |

# Grammar glossary

main verb | adjective | modal auxiliary | adverb | article | pronoun | main verb

**Learn these useful words and you can understand more about the language you are studying.**

noun | pronoun | main verb | preposition | noun | auxiliary verb

**Combinations** refers to words that frequently occur together.
For example: *common sense   get along well   Happy Birthday*

**Expressions** are groups of words that belong together where the words and word order never or rarely change.
For example: ***black and white   That reminds me**, I have to buy some toothpaste.*
***How do you do?***

**Objects** usually come after the verb and show who or what is affected by the verb.
For example: *She closed **the window**.   My neighbor hates **me**.   I made **a pot of coffee**.*

**Particles** are adverbs or prepositions that form part of a phrasal verb.
For example: *sit **down**   switch **off**   look **after***

**Phrasal verbs** are verbs consisting of a main verb + particle(s). Phrasal verbs are sometimes referred to as two- or three-word verbs.
For example: ***find out**   Please **take** your shoes **off**.*
*I sometimes **take care of** my neighbor's pet.*

**Subjects** usually come before the verb and refer to the main person or thing you are talking about.
For example: ***Money** doesn't grow on trees.   **My tailor** is rich.*
***The biggest rock group in the world** has started a world tour.*

# Classroom language

## The classroom

What's that in English?
What's this in English?
answer  bag  board  book  cassette/CD player  chair  definition  desk  dictionary  door
map  pen  picture  piece of paper  question  sentence  student  teacher  window  word

## Teacher language

Work with a partner/in groups of three.
Look at the board/photograph.
Listen to the conversation/song.
Write the answers/your name on a piece of paper.
Read the text/article.
Use your dictionary/a piece of paper.

## Student language

How do you say… in English?
How do you spell it?
Can you repeat that?
I don't understand.
What does… mean?

# Numbers

| | | | |
|---|---|---|---|
| 0 | zero | 16 | sixteen |
| 1 | one | 17 | seventeen |
| 2 | two | 18 | eighteen |
| 3 | three | 19 | nineteen |
| 4 | four | 20 | twenty |
| 5 | five | 21 | twenty-one |
| 6 | six | 30 | thirty |
| 7 | seven | 40 | forty |
| 8 | eight | 50 | fifty |
| 9 | nine | 60 | sixty |
| 10 | ten | 70 | seventy |
| 11 | eleven | 80 | eighty |
| 12 | twelve | 90 | ninety |
| 13 | thirteen | 100 | a hundred |
| 14 | fourteen | 1,000 | a thousand |
| 15 | fifteen | 1,000,000 | a million |

# Phonetic symbols

## VOWELS

| | | |
|---|---|---|
| /ɪ/ | big fish | /bɪg fɪʃ/ |
| /i/ | green beans | /grin binz/ |
| /ʊ/ | should look | /ʃʊd lʊk/ |
| /u/ | blue moon | /blu mun/ |
| /ɛ/ | ten eggs | /tɛn ɛgz/ |
| /ə/ | about mother | /əbaʊt mʌðər/ |
| /æ/ | fat cat | /fæt kæt/ |
| /ʌ/ | must come | /mʌst kʌm/ |
| /ɔ/ | fall ball | /fɔl bɔl/ |
| /ɑ/ | hot spot | /hɑt spɑt/ |

## DIPHTHONGS

| | | |
|---|---|---|
| /ei/ | face | /feis/ |
| /ɔi/ | boy | /bɔi/ |
| /ou/ | nose | /nouz/ |
| /ɑi/ | eye | /ɑi/ |
| /ɑu/ | mouth | /mɑuθ/ |

## CONSONANTS

| | | |
|---|---|---|
| /p/ | pen | /pɛn/ |
| /b/ | bad | /bæd/ |
| /t/ | tea | /ti/ |
| /d/ | dog | /dɔg/ |
| /tʃ/ | church | /tʃɔrtʃ/ |
| /dʒ/ | jazz | /dʒæz/ |
| /k/ | cost | /kɔst/ |
| /g/ | girl | /gɔrl/ |
| /f/ | far | /fɑr/ |
| /v/ | voice | /vɔis/ |
| /θ/ | thin | /θɪn/ |
| /ð/ | then | /ðɛn/ |
| /s/ | snake | /snɛik/ |
| /z/ | noise | /nɔiz/ |
| /ʃ/ | shop | /ʃɑp/ |
| /ʒ/ | measure | /mɛʒər/ |
| /m/ | make | /mɛik/ |
| /n/ | nine | /nɑin/ |
| /ŋ/ | sing | /sɪŋ/ |
| /h/ | house | /hɑus/ |
| /l/ | leg | /lɛg/ |
| /r/ | red | /rɛd/ |
| /w/ | wet | /wɛt/ |
| /y/ | yes | /yɛs/ |

## STRESS

In this book, word stress is shown by underlining the stressed syllable.
For example: <u>wa</u>ter; re<u>sult</u>; disa<u>ppo</u>inting

## LETTERS OF THE ALPHABET

| /ei/ | /i/ | /ɛ/ | /ɑi/ | /ou/ | /u/ | /ɑr/ |
|---|---|---|---|---|---|---|
| Aa | Bb | Ff | Ii | Oo | Qq | Rr |
| Hh | Cc | Ll | Yy | | Uu | |
| Jj | Dd | Mm | | | Ww | |
| Kk | Ee | Nn | | | | |
| | Gg | Ss | | | | |
| | Pp | Xx | | | | |
| | Tt | | | | | |
| | Vv | | | | | |
| | Zz | | | | | |

# Irregular verbs

| Simple form | Simple past | Past participle |
|---|---|---|
| be | was/were | been |
| beat | beat | beaten |
| become | became | become |
| begin | began | begun |
| bend | bent | bent |
| bet | bet | bet |
| bite | bit | bitten |
| blow | blew | blown |
| break | broke | broken |
| bring | brought | brought |
| build | built | built |
| burn | burned | burned |
| burst | burst | burst |
| buy | bought | bought |
| can | could | (been able) |
| catch | caught | caught |
| choose | chose | chosen |
| come | came | come |
| cost | cost | cost |
| cut | cut | cut |
| deal | dealt | dealt |
| do | did | done |
| draw | drew | drawn |
| dream | dreamed | dreamed |
| drink | drank | drunk |
| drive | drove | driven |
| eat | ate | eaten |
| fall | fell | fallen |
| feed | fed | fed |
| feel | felt | felt |
| fight | fought | fought |
| find | found | found |
| fly | flew | flown |
| forget | forgot | forgotten |
| forgive | forgave | forgiven |
| freeze | froze | frozen |
| get | got | gotten |
| give | gave | given |
| go | went | gone |
| grow | grew | grown |
| hang | hung/hanged | hung/hanged |
| have | had | had |
| hear | heard | heard |
| hide | hid | hidden |
| hit | hit | hit |
| hold | held | held |
| hurt | hurt | hurt |
| keep | kept | kept |
| kneel | knelt/kneeled | knelt/kneeled |
| know | knew | known |
| lay | laid | laid |
| lead | led | led |
| learn | learned | learned |
| leave | left | left |
| lend | lent | lent |
| let | let | let |

| Simple form | Simple past | Past participle |
|---|---|---|
| lie | lay/lied | lain/lied |
| light | lit/lighted | lit/lighted |
| lose | lost | lost |
| make | made | made |
| mean | meant | meant |
| meet | met | met |
| must | had to | (had to) |
| pay | paid | paid |
| put | put | put |
| read | read /red/ | read /red/ |
| ride | rode | ridden |
| ring | rang | rung |
| rise | rose | risen |
| run | ran | run |
| say | said | said |
| see | saw | seen |
| sell | sold | sold |
| send | sent | sent |
| set | set | set |
| shake | shook | shaken |
| shine | shined/shone | shined/shone |
| shoot | shot | shot |
| show | showed | shown |
| shrink | shrank | shrunk |
| shut | shut | shut |
| sing | sang | sung |
| sink | sank | sunk |
| sit | sat | sat |
| sleep | slept | slept |
| slide | slid | slid |
| smell | smelled | smelled |
| speak | spoke | spoken |
| spell | spelled | spelled |
| spend | spent | spent |
| spill | spilled | spilled |
| split | split | split |
| spoil | spoiled | spoiled |
| spread | spread | spread |
| stand | stood | stood |
| steal | stole | stolen |
| stick | stuck | stuck |
| swear | swore | sworn |
| swell | swelled | swollen/swelled |
| swim | swam | swum |
| take | took | taken |
| teach | taught | taught |
| tear | tore | torn |
| tell | told | told |
| think | thought | thought |
| throw | threw | thrown |
| understand | understood | understood |
| wake | woke | woken |
| wear | wore | worn |
| win | won | won |
| write | wrote | written |

# Tapescripts

## Unit 11

🔊 59

Albert is Jimmy's father. They have the same smile.
Andy is Nancy's father. They have the same mouth.
Sue is Will's mother. Will looks like Sue.
Jennifer is Carla's mother. They have the same nose.
Gus and Ellen are brother and sister. They have the same dark eyes.

🔊 60

(I = Interviewer; S = Stuart)
I: Stuart, you really like buying clothes, don't you?
S: Oh, yes, I love it.
I: How many items of clothing do you have?
S: Well…I have 350 shirts. I wear three or four different shirts every day.
I: What???…Uh…Who does the laundry?
S: My wife does the laundry, and I do the ironing. Then I have 200 suits.
I like bright colors—red, blue, green.
I: Mm, I see.
S: Then I have 150 pairs of pants and 125 pairs of shoes.
I: Stuart, why do you have so many clothes?
S: Well, it's my hobby. Some people spend thousands of dollars on cars or vacations. I don't have a car, and I never go on vacation. I buy clothes.

🔊 61

(See page 48.)

🔊 62

**Conversation a**
A: How many hats do you have?
B: Fourteen.
A: Forty?
B: No, fourteen.
A: Oh, fourteen.

**Conversation b**
A: How many ties do you have?
B: Nineteen.
A: Ninety?
B: No, nineteen.
A: Oh, nineteen.

**Conversation c**
A: How many rings do you have?
B: Fifteen.
A: Fifty?
B: No, fifteen.
A: Oh, fifteen.

**Conversation d**
A: How many T-shirts do you have?
B: Thirty.
A: Thirty?
B: Yes, thirty.
A: Oh, O.K.

🔊 63

Good evening. I'm Ross White, and I'm standing outside the Hollywood Theater, and I'm waiting for the big stars to arrive for this year's Oscar ceremony.
    And here comes Penelope Jones. She's wearing a beautiful blue dress.
    Oh, wow—there's Melanie Matthews. She's getting out of her car now—she's wearing a very short dress. Yes, very nice.
    Oh, look! There's Kerry Fisher. She's wearing a white suit and red boots. What's she doing? Oh, she's waving to her fans. That's nice. Such a big star, but she loves her fans.
    Bobby Finn is arriving now. Oh, he's so good-looking! And who is that woman? He's holding her hand. She's lovely—she's wearing a long white dress.

🔊 64

**a)**
"Are you wearing jeans?"
"Yes, I am."
"No, I'm not."

**b)**
"Are you sitting next to a window?"
"Yes, I am."
"No, I'm not."

**c)**
"Is your teacher standing up?"
"Yes, she is."
"No, she isn't."

**d)**
"Is the traffic making noise?"
"Yes, it is."
"No, it isn't."

**e)**
"Are the birds singing outside?"
"Yes, they are."
"No, they're not."

**f)**
"Are you having a good time?"
"Yes, I am."
"No, I'm not."

## Unit 12

🔊 65

About eight weeks after she made her dream book, Glenna was driving down a California freeway. Suddenly a gorgeous red-and-white Cadillac passed her. She looked at the car because it was a beautiful car. And the driver looked at her and smiled, and she smiled back. He followed her for the next fifteen miles. He parked, she parked…and eventually she married him.

After their first date, Jim sent Glenna a dozen roses. They dated for two years, and every Monday morning she received a red rose.
    Then she found out that Jim had a hobby. His hobby was collecting diamonds.
    They had the traditional wedding Glenna wanted, and Jim chose their honeymoon destination—it was St. John's Island in the Caribbean. Then they moved into their beautiful new home.
    Glenna didn't tell Jim about the dream book for almost a year after they got married.
    Eight months after she created her dream book, Glenna became vice president of human resources in the company where she worked—it was her dream job.
    This sounds like a fairy tale, but it's a true story.

🔊 66

**1**
A: Next question. On the border of which two South American countries can you find Iguaçu Falls?
B: Oh. Uh. Mm, I know this one. Is it Argentina and Chile? No—Argentina and Brazil.
A: Is that your final answer?
B: Yes.
A: Are you sure?
B: Uh, yes.
A: Carol, I asked you where you can find Iguaçu Falls. Your answer was on the border of Argentina and Brazil. It's the correct answer. You've just won 125,000 dollars!!!

**2**
Plenty of sunshine today. Temperatures up to 70 degrees. And tomorrow is going to be another beautiful day. There may be some clouds in the northeast, but generally a warm and sunny day.

**3**
That's it! They've done it! The Florida Marlins are the new champions! They beat the New York Yankees 2–0 in game 6 of the World Series!

**4**
Police arrested two men after they attempted to rob a bank on Wall Street this morning. The men were armed, but nobody was hurt.

**5**
A: Oh hello, Jessica. How are you today?
B: Oh, my life is over! Did you hear about Andy?
A: No. Tell me!
B: Well, I heard he's going to marry Rachel.
A: Rachel Smedley—oh, no!

**6**

A: Well, Michael, you've had a very successful career in the movie business. Did you always want to be a movie star?

B: Not exactly. I grew up on a farm in Nebraska, and when I was a young boy, all I wanted to be was a farmer like my dad.

A: So what made you change your mind?

B: Well, it was…

**7**

The shark is the king of the sea. It fills people with fear. But that's not the whole story. Yes, some kinds of shark are dangerous, but most of them are harmless and shy. Take the spotted wobbegong—not a beautiful specimen—pretty ugly, in fact…

**8**

A: Anybody want some coffee?

B: Yeah, O.K.

Big Brother: This is Big Brother. Will Lynne please come to the Diary Room immediately?

B: Ooh, I wonder what that's all about?

A: Dunno. Do you want sugar in your coffee?

**67**

(D = Danielle; L = Lynne)

D: Lynne, congratulations. How do you feel?

L: Oh, great. I feel fantastic. I'm so happy.

D: What's the first thing you're going to do when you get out?

L: I'm going to have a big party for all my friends. I missed them so much.

D: O.K. What are you going to do with the money?

L: Well, I'm going to give some of it to charity, and with the rest I'm going to buy a house for my mom.

D: So, which of your *Big Brother* housemates are you going to see again?

L: There are some people I'd like to see again, and there are two people I'm definitely not going to see again. I think you know who they are.

D: Yes, of course. That was really horrible. But your hair looks O.K. now.

L: Yeah, well…

D: Anyway Lynne, the question everyone wants to ask. You and Eddie became really good—uh—friends in the House. So are you going to see Eddie again?

L: Well, I don't know. Yes, of course we're going to *see* each other. But we don't know what's going to happen.

D: What advice would you give to future *Big Brother* contestants?

L: Don't do it! No, I'm just kidding. Be yourself, and be patient. It's very boring in there.

D: Finally, Lynne, what are your future plans?

L: Well, first I'm going to go out and spend some money. Then I want to start my singing career. I'm going to record a CD. Actually, I'd really like to be a TV personality.

D: Oh—well, good luck.

**68**

(See page 53.)

**69**

(See page 53.)

# Unit 13

**70**

(LFC = Lost and Found clerk; J = Judy)

LFC: Lost and Found. How can I help you?

J: Oh, uh, hello…I'm calling because I lost my bag yesterday.

LFC: I see. Well, we received thirty-eight bags yesterday. What color is it, and what's it made of?

J: Oh, yes, uh…it's black, and it's made of leather.

LFC: Hm…black…leather…I have twenty-four black leather bags here. Can you give me some more information?

J: Oh, dear. Yes. Uh, it has a zipper in the front and a long strap.

LFC: Does it have any pockets on the front?

J: No, but there's a pocket on the side for a cellphone.

LFC: O.K., how big is it?

J: It's pretty big—I wear it over my shoulder.

LFC: So what kind of bag is it? A shoulder bag?

J: Yes, a shoulder bag. That's right.

LFC: Is there anything in it?

J: Yes, there's an address book and some keys. Oh, and Hissy.

LFC: Hissy?

J: Yes, Hissy the snake.

LFC: There's a snake…in your bag?

J: Yes, but don't worry, it's made of plastic. It belongs to my five-year-old son.

LFC: I see. Well, I think we have your bag here. The office is open from nine in the morning…

**71**

Think about the last time you went shopping.
Where and when did you go shopping?
What did you want to buy?
How long did you spend shopping?
Did you get what you wanted?
How much money did you spend?
How did you pay?
Did you enjoy your shopping trip?

**72**

(See page 56.)

**73**

a) Sixty-six thousand, one hundred twelve.

b) One hundred ninety-four thousand, four hundred fifty-nine.

c) Twenty-five thousand.

d) One hundred fifty-seven thousand, nine hundred forty-seven.

e) One million, nine hundred eighteen thousand, three hundred eighty-seven.

f) Three hundred twenty-four thousand, one hundred eighty-eight.

**74**

1 The most valuable bikini was valued at $194,459. The hand-made, diamond-encrusted bikini was made in 2000.

2 The most valuable watch was in 18-carat gold, made by Patek Phillippe in 1922. A collector from the Middle East bought it for $1,918,387 in 1999.

3 Levi Strauss and Co. bought a 100-year-old pair of Levi jeans from a private collector for $25,000 in 1997.

4 The dress that Judy Garland wore in the 1939 production of *The Wizard of Oz* was auctioned for $324,188 in 1999.

5 The owner of the Las Vegas Hard Rock Hotel bought Geri Halliwell's Union Jack dress for $66,112 in 1998. She wore it for a Spice Girls' performance in 1997.

6 The boxing robe Mohammed Ali wore before his so-called "Rumble in the Jungle" fight with George Foreman in 1974 was sold for $157,947 in a 1997 Beverly Hills sale.

# Unit 14

**75**

(See page 58.)

**76**

a) Bend your knees.
b) Cross your legs.
c) Fold your arms.
d) Nod your head.
e) Clap your hands.
f) Stamp your feet.
g) Snap your fingers.
h) Shrug your shoulders.

**77**

(See page 60.)

**78**

(D = Danny; L = Louise)

D: Do you want to come to the gym later?

L: Oh, no thanks. I can't. I'm too tired.

D: Well, you should exercise. It gives you more energy.

L: It's not just that—I have too much work. And I have a bad back.

D: That's because you sit at your computer all day. You should go swimming—swimming is really good for your back.

L: I hate swimming—the swimming pool is too crowded—and anyway, I have a cold.

D: A cold? Oh, too bad. Maybe you should go away for a few days.

L: Yes, I know, but I don't have enough money to go away.

D: Look, you seem to be in a bad mood. Do you want to go out tomorrow night? We can go clubbing.

L: No, I can't go dancing. My foot hurts.

D: Too tired? A bad back? 104A cold? And your foot hurts? Hey, Louise—I think you need a new body.

# Unit 15

🔊 79

A: camera, curly, earring, island, lovely, neighbor, pushy, selfish, stomach
B: alcohol, exercise, favorite, generous
C: appointments, collector, contestant, impulsive, performance, successful

🔊 80

Think about someone you think is good-looking. It can be someone you know or a famous person.
What's his or her name?
What does he or she do?
How old is he or she?
What color hair does he or she have?
What style is it?
What color eyes does he or she have?
What other features does he or she have?
What kind of clothes does he or she wear?
What do you think he or she is doing now?

🔊 81

(See page 65.)

# Unit 16

🔊 82

(T = Tom; M = Mom)
T: Hello.
M: Hello, Tom.
T: Oh hi, Mom. Are you O.K.?
M: Fine, thanks. But I need some help with my new computer.
T: Oh—do you want to surf the Net?
M: No, I just want to send an e-mail to Carol.
T: O.K. That's no problem. First, find the e-mail icon.
M: Icon? What's an icon?
T: It's a little picture, like a symbol.
M: Where is it?
T: It's on your desktop.
M: Well, there's nothing on my desk.
T: No, Mom, your desktop is on your computer screen.
M: Oh. Well, I can see lots of little pictures there.
T: Right. You need to click on the e-mail icon.
M: Click?
T: Press the button on your mouse.
M: Mouse?
T: THE THING IN YOUR HAND.
M: Oh, yes. O.K, I've done that.
T: Now, click on the new message icon and type Carol's e-mail address in the box that says "to."
M: O.K.
T: Then type your message in the box and call me back.
M: O.K. Bye.

🔊 83

(T = Tom/Thomas; M = Mom)
T: Yes, hello, Mom.
M: I'm ready to send that e-mail.
T: O.K. To send the message, you need to go online.
M: Online?
T: Yes, you need to connect to the Internet.
M: Oh, right. I knew that.
T: Now, at the top of your screen, there's a toolbar. Click on the "Send and receive" icon, and this will connect you to the Net through your modem.
M: Oh, Thomas, speak English! I don't understand computer language.
T: Oh, I don't believe this. O.K., what can you see at the top of your screen?
M: Well, there are lots of little pictures and…

🔊 84

(D = Darren; N = Nick)
D: Nick?
N: Darren! Wow, you haven't changed at all.
D: And you look exactly the same—good to see you.
N: Wow, I can't believe it—after eleven years.
D: Yeah. Have you heard from any other friends from school?
N: Yes, a couple of people—that Friends Reunited Web site is great.
D: Hey, do you have that list?
N: Yes, here it is.
D: Oh yes, I remember—"10 things to do before we're 30." Well, we're 29—how many things have *you* done?
N: Not many—three, I think. I've gone snowboarding, and I've gone bungee jumping, and I've visited John Lennon's grave in New York. And that's it really. What about you?
D: Let's see—I haven't recorded a CD—I stopped playing music when I finished school.
N: Yeah, me too.
D: And I've been to a U2 concert, but I haven't met any of them.
N: Have you traveled much?
D: Well, I've been to South America three times.
N: Wow!
D: But I haven't been to the Himalayas yet, or Egypt.
N: Have you ever been snowboarding?
D: Yes, I've done that. But I haven't gone bungee jumping. I haven't made a lot of money, either—I'm a teacher!
N: Well, I've made a lot of money, but I've spent it. Anyway, have you met the love of your life?
D: No, I haven't met anyone special yet. How about you?
N: Yes, I forgot to tell you. I'm married to Pamela.
D: Pamela?
N: Yes, you know, the gorgeous singer in our band.

🔊 85

a)
"Have you ever visited the Web site for your high school?"
"Yes, I have."
"No, I haven't."

b)
"Has your school ever tried to get in touch with you?"
"Yes, it has."
"No, it hasn't."

c)
"Have you ever gone to a high school reunion?"
"Yes, I have."
"No, I haven't."

d)
"Have you ever received an e-mail from an old friend?"
"Yes, I have."
"No, I haven't."

e)
"Have your parents ever sent you an e-mail?"
"Yes, they have."
"No, they haven't."

f)
"Have you ever met somebody new on the Internet?"
"Yes, I have."
"No, I haven't."

🔊 86

Think about an old friend you would like to get in touch with.
What's his or her name?
Where did you first meet?
How old were you?
Why did you become friends?
What kinds of things did you talk about?
What kinds of things did you do together?
What is your best memory of him or her?
When was the last time you saw him or her?
Why would you like to get in touch with him or her?

# Unit 17

🔊 87

(R = Reporter; M1, 2, 3 = Men;
W1, 2, 3 = Women)

R: This is City Radio. My name is Andy Cowle. Earlier, we asked people on the street, "What drives you crazy on the road?" Here are some of their answers.
1
M1: I can't stand it when people drive very slowly. They usually go out on the weekend—you know, Sunday drivers—and they drive very slowly on country roads, where it's impossible to pass them.

**2**

W1: I hate it when people double-park their cars on busy city streets. Other cars can't get past them!

**3**

M2: I hate it when drivers signal to turn left...and then they turn right!...or go straight ahead! It's so dangerous!

**4**

W2: Well, I don't like getting stuck in traffic. In my city, rush hour in the morning, and in the evening, is awful. I try to work at home as much as possible.

**5**

M3: Construction drives me crazy, especially on the highway. You go on the highway to save time, and then you get stuck in traffic because of the construction.

**6**

W3: It drives me crazy when people use their cellphones in the car. I almost had an accident last week because this woman was talking on her phone and she didn't see the traffic light turn red. She almost killed me.

**88**

first, second, third, fourth, fifth, sixth, seventh, eighth, ninth, tenth

**89**

1  Your starting point is A1. Go straight, take the third right, the second left, and go straight. Where are you?
2  Your starting point is A2. Take the first left, the first right, the fifth right, and the first left. Where are you?
3  Your starting point is A3. Go straight, take the fourth left, the second right, and go straight. Where are you?

# Unit 18

**90**

(See page 74.)

**91**

**a)**
"Were you living in the same house this time last year?"
"Yes, I was."
"No, I wasn't."

**b)**
"Were your parents watching TV at 11:30 last night?"
"Yes, they were."
"No, they weren't."

**c)**
"Were you studying in your English class this time yesterday?"
"Yes, I was."
"No, I wasn't."

**d)**
"Was it raining when you woke up this morning?"
"Yes, it was."
"No, it wasn't."

**e)**
"Were you wearing a hat when you went out this morning?"
"Yes, I was."
"No, I wasn't."

**f)**
"Were you speaking English when the class started?"
"Yes, I was."
"No, I wasn't."

**92**

**The Princess and the Frog**
Have you ever heard the story of the princess and the frog?
Well, once upon a time, there was a princess. She was beautiful, confident, and independent.
She lived in a castle in a country far away.
One day, she was sitting near a pond in the grounds of her castle. She was thinking about her life.
There she met a frog.
The frog said to her, "Beautiful princess, I was once a handsome prince. But then an evil witch changed me into a frog. Kiss me and I will turn back into a handsome, young prince. Then, my darling, we can get married and live in your castle with my mother. You can prepare my meals, wash my clothes, and take care of my children."
Later, as the princess was enjoying a meal of frog legs in a delicious cream sauce, she smiled and thought to herself, "Thanks, my prince...but no, thanks."

# Unit 19

**93, 94, 95**

(See page 78.)

**96**

**a)**
"Was your house built before 1980?"
"Yes, it was."
"No, it wasn't."

**b)**
"Were your shoes designed in Italy?"
"Yes, they were."
"No, they weren't."

**c)**
"Is your salary paid by check?"
"Yes, it is."
"No, it isn't."

**d)**
"Were you invited to any parties last week?"
"Yes, I was."
"No, I wasn't."

**e)**
"Is your name spelled the same way in English?"
"Yes, it is."
"No, it isn't."

**f)**
"Was your cellphone made in Japan?"
"Yes, it was."
"No, it wasn't."

**97**

**New York in the Winter**
Today will start off very wet with temperatures between 35 and 40 degrees Fahrenheit.
It will be cloudy in the afternoon, and there will probably be snow later on. It will be overcast all day.
Tomorrow will be the same, and the next day, and the day after.
Next week might be a little sunnier, but not much.

**98**

I like October. It's fall in Japan. Yes, fall is my favorite time of year. In Kyoto the weather is beautiful in October. It's warm but not hot. In the summer it's too hot—I hate it—but in October, the temperature is perfect.
Also, the countryside is very colorful at that time of year. The trees are red and orange. We have a name for this in Japan – it's called "koyo"—it means the changing color of the trees in the fall. I usually wear light clothes—T-shirts and dresses. You don't need a coat when you go out. It's lovely.
Of course, October is not vacation time, but on weekends we go for walks in the hills and we have picnics. We enjoy looking at the countryside at that time of year.
I like that time of year because it's beautiful. Yes, I think Kyoto is the best place in the world at that time of year.

# Unit 20

**99**

(See page 82)

**100**

And here are the words for tonight's bingo.
meant, meant  caught, caught
slept, slept  worn, worn  made, made
woken, woken  done, done
brought, brought  shot, shot  had, had
spent, spent  paid, paid  kept, kept
felt, felt  broken, broken  fallen, fallen
thought, thought  found, found
lent, lent  spoken, spoken  eaten, eaten
written, written  sat, sat  met, met
taught, taught  read, read  heard, heard
driven, driven  sold, sold  built, built

## 101

A Hollywood director was shooting an important movie in the desert when an old Native American man came up to him and said, "Tomorrow rain."

The next day it rained.

A few days later, the director was talking to the cameraman about the next day's shooting. The Native American went up to him and said, "Tomorrow storm."

He was right again, and he saved the director thousands of dollars.

The director was very impressed and gave the old man a job.

The old man continued to predict the weather correctly, but then he didn't come for three weeks.

The director was planning to shoot an important scene, and he needed good weather. So he went to look for the Native American.

When he found the old man, he said, "Listen, I have to shoot an important scene tomorrow. What will the weather be like?"

The old man shook his head and said, "Don't know. Radio broken."

## 102

Think about a trip that you often took
    when you were younger.
Where did your trip start and finish?
How far was it?
How did you travel?
What time did you usually start out?
How long did it take you?
What kind of terrain did you go through?
What kinds of buildings did you go past?
Who did you usually travel with?
What did you usually do on your trip?
When was the last time you took this trip?